The Dawn of Flame-Beings: Mythological Musings Based on a Cosmology of Light

PRAVIR MALIK, PH.D.

ILLUSTRATIONS: MARGARET ASTRID PHANES

Copyright © 2023 Pravir Malik
All rights reserved.

ISBN-13: 979-8-9862443-3-4

"Built is the golden tower, the flame-child born."

(Sri Aurobindo, *Savitri*)

AUTHOR'S INTRODUCTION	**6**

PART 1: DARK BEGINNINGS — 8

#1: AN INTRODUCTION	9
#2: LIGHT AS CREATOR	11
#3: THE DARK BOSOM	14
#4: THE TITAN REIGN	17
#5: FORBIDDEN LOVE	19
#6: TITAN MATTER	22
#7: THE DARK PRALAYA	25
#8: HIDDEN KNOWLEDGE	28
#9: THE LAST PRALAYA	30

PART 2: MYSTERIES OF LIGHT — 32

#10: THE SECRET OF C	33
#11: C-WORLD EMBRYO	36
#12: THE BIRTH OF SPACE-TIME-ENERGY-GRAVITY	38
#13: THE EVER-PRESENT PRIEST	40
#14: THE EDGE OF LIGHT	43
#15: THE CRUCIBLE OF LOVE	45
#16: THE FIRST OF THE MULTIVERSE MYSTERIES	47
#17: THE WONDER OF ATOMIC-EQUILIBRIA	49
#18: THE ESSENCE OF LIFE	51
#19: THE MIRACLE OF THE CELL	53

PART 3: THE MAKING OF HISTORY — 55

#20: THE INEVITABLE BATTLE	56
#21: THE VANITY OF THE STRANGLE-HOLD	58
#22: THE GIFT	60
#23: PIONEERS OF LIGHT	62
#24: SHE	64
#25: HE	66
#26: THE DESTINED COURTSHIP	68
#27: THE ENVISIONING OF EARTH	70
#28: EARTH	73
#29: EARTH-FLAME'S ODE TO INFINITY	75
#30: THE VERITABLE CREATORS OF HISTORY	77
#31: THE GREATEST OF HISTORICAL EVENTS	79

PART 4: THE DAWN OF FLAME-BEINGS — 81

#32: FLAME-BEING'S MATTER	82
#33: THE NEW ERA OF BEING-POSSIBILITY	84
#34: UNLIKELY MARRIAGES	86
#35: GALACTIC COLONIZATION	88
#36: EARTH'S COSMIC TREE OF LIGHT	90
#37: THE ONCE EXISTING TREE OF LIFE	92
#38: ONCE-TYPAL WORLDS	94
#39: THE VERITABLE MATERIAL HOLIDAY	96

PART 5: THE NEW COSMOS — 98

#40: SPACE-TIME-ENERGY-GRAVITY MOUNDS	99
#41: AMOREM PARTICLES	101
#42: 108,000 FUNCTION-FOLDEDNESS ATOMIC-EQUILIBRIA	103
#43: LOVE-FOUND CELLS	105
#44: FRACTAL FULLNESS	107
#45: THE SURRENDER OF QUANTA AND THE BEING OF SPEED	110
#46: MATTER'S ROLE IN EMPRESS-EMPEROR-HOOD	113
#47: HE & SHE	115
#48: INFINITESIMAL MATERIAL UNIVERSES	117
#49: INEXPRESSIBLE DOMAINS OF LIGHT	119
#50: THE MARCH OF MATTER'S MYSTERY	121

RELEVANT BACKGROUND AND FOLLOW-UP INFORMATION — 123

THE AUTHOR'S EARLY BOOKS	123
THE FRACTAL SERIES	123
THE COSMOLOGY OF LIGHT SERIES	123
THE APPLICATION OF COSMOLOGY OF LIGHT SERIES	123
THE ARTISTIC INTERPRETATION OF COSMOLOGY OF LIGHT SERIES	124
NOTE ON GENESIS OF BOOKS	125
ABOUT THE AUTHOR	127
ABOUT THE ILLUSTRATOR	128
SELECTED AUTHOR ONLINE PRESENCE	128

Author's Introduction

The Dawn of Flame-Beings is built on the ten-book *Cosmology of Light* series.

This original series was based on a simple exploration: why does light travel at the constant speed of c - 186,000 miles per second – in vacuum? This exploration led to the consideration of the intentionality of c, and to the consideration of light existing at other constant speeds ranging from infinity to zero. Each constant speed of light was imagined creating a distinct world or layer in which space, time, materialization, and other dynamics were uniquely emergent and operated differently. The interaction of five layers of light existing at different constant speeds was then mathematically modeled to explain all the past, diversity, possibility, and future of known material life.

In the course of the mathematical modeling many unique beings and becomings were glimpsed – a mysterious creator with an eye that flashed light, a contrary beginning manifest as a dark bosom, titans, pralayas, world-embryos, a macro space-time-energy-gravity fourfoldness and its micro-counterpart the ever-present priest, battles between original darkness and forever emerging light, powerful meta and multi-function feminine and masculine aspects of the mysterious creator embodied as a She and a He, the earth as the place of an extraordinary courtship between them, the end of death, the birth of flame-beings, the growth and spreading of earth's cosmic tree of light supplanting an original tree of life, the growth of flame-beings to far exceed their human origins in extraordinary ways, the seeding of new flame-being star-clusters, the changing of typal into evolutionary worlds, the birth of new quantum particles, new atoms, new molecular plans allowing Love to materially reveal more of its fullness, the glorious reign of matter one with spirit, the changing of cosmos, the continuous and fuller births of that original mystery manifesting in an unending display of splendor.

In other words, a full mythology was glimpsed in the cosmology of light, and in *The Dawn of Flame-Beings* abstract and impersonal mathematical and scientific concepts have been personified to begin to materialize powers and forces and entities integral to the history and future of the earth and cosmos.

In this process of making sense of the past and extrapolating into the future a much greater foundation than the *Cosmology of Light* was tapped into: Sri Aurobindo's epic *Savitri*. About *Savitri*, The Mother, Sri Aurobindo's counterpart has said:

> "*Savitri*, the prophetic vision of the world's history, including the announcement of the earth's future", and

"*Savitri* The supreme revelation of Sri Aurobindo's vision".

Many insights into the action of He and She, earth and death and love, the changing of matter based on a foundation of light, the birth of the flame-child, the history and future of the earth are revealed in *Savitri*.

An interpretation of these insights has guided the mythology in *The Dawn of Flame-Beings*. A mythology is by its nature vast and would require volumes and volumes to do it justice. Instead, this book has only the bare beginnings and has been expressed as a series of musings accompanied by meditative illustrations to allow the reader to penetrate more deeply into the mythology.

The book has been arranged in five parts: Dark Beginnings, Mysteries of Light, The Making of History, The Dawn of Flame-Beings, and The New Cosmos.

While the first three parts have to do with earth's past spread over billions of years and multiple projections of cosmos returning to and finally breaking away from some dark origin due to varied action by personified actors ranging from the big bang to a quantum-particle multi-verse to a fourfold cellular foundation for life allowing death to be overcome in a culmination of history, amongst others, the fourth and fifth part have to do with a possible future built from a transformed cell in which the infinity of light continues to find new and extraordinary pathways to express itself in flame-beings who are powerful and loving enough to transform all cosmos.

I hope these mythological musings may allow more visceral entrance into the possibilities embodied by a cosmology of light.

Pravir Malik,
San Francisco

Part 1: Dark Beginnings

#1: An Introduction

The **Cosmology of Light** has been constructed by imagining light to exist at multiple constant speeds simultaneously. The starting point of this exploration, simply, is why does light travel at the constant speed of c? And the answer, from a Cosmology of Light perspective, is that this is intentional. It is required so that our cosmos would emerge in the way that it has, with the possibilities resident within it. These are themes I have explored in **three different ways** over the last few years, and it has surfaced unique interpretations and approaches to a vast range of subjects from the meaning of quanta to the **significance of Euler's Identity**, to the **design of a different type of quantum computer**, to the **future of technology development**, to approaches to World Peace, amongst many others.

But here I want to begin a short series as it relates to mythology. A Cosmology of Light offers a view into some of the most basic questions encapsulated by any mythology — how creation began, what is its purpose, what is good and what is evil, why is the human condition the way it is, and so on — of course, all presented through story. Through going deeper into the nature and play of light there is a whole genre of stories, a whole mythology, that can arise. This is what I seek to tease out in this series.

I am not going to get into the creation of stories based on light. Instead, I am going to focus on kernels that can serve as the basis for endless stories based on viewing light as has been done in a Cosmology of Light.

#2: Light as Creator

In the **introductory piece** to this series, it was suggested that the known speed with which light travels, c, is an intentionality. But before mythology associated with c can be surfaced, the contextual mythology to do with that which creates has first to be explored.

A Creator is often thought to be all-powerful, all-present, all-knowledgeable, at the least. In considering light in an infinitely fast state, we can get a glimpse into the emergence of such properties.

Imagine, therefore, a large volume with a light source at the center. Because it travels infinitely fast it will be present in that volume instantaneously. So, it will be all-present or *omnipresent*. Since anything that appears or disappears will be recorded in the substance of the all-present light, the light will have full knowledge of everything that is happening in it. That is, it will be all-knowledgeable, or *omniscient*. If anything not of the nature of light were to arise, sooner or later it will be overcome or subsumed by the nature of light, and hence light will be all-powerful or *omnipotent*. Since everything will be connected in the all-present fiber of light there will be an implicit harmony that would prevail and hence light would be all-harmonious or *omniharmonious*.

So light existing in some native state such that it has infinite speed can be seen to be omnipresent, omniscient, omnipotent, omniharmonious.

But another way to think of this is that if there were something that was omnipresent, omniscient, omnipotent, omniharmonious, it would be self-illuminative by dint of knowing itself and powerfully creating in itself as per principles of implicit harmony. But this is what Light is.

Perhaps it is the case then that some original Mystery decided to create. This manifests as the opening of an Eye. With that opening Light flashes forth. Flashing forth infinitely fast it is endowed with omnipresence, omnipotence, omniscience, and omniharmony.

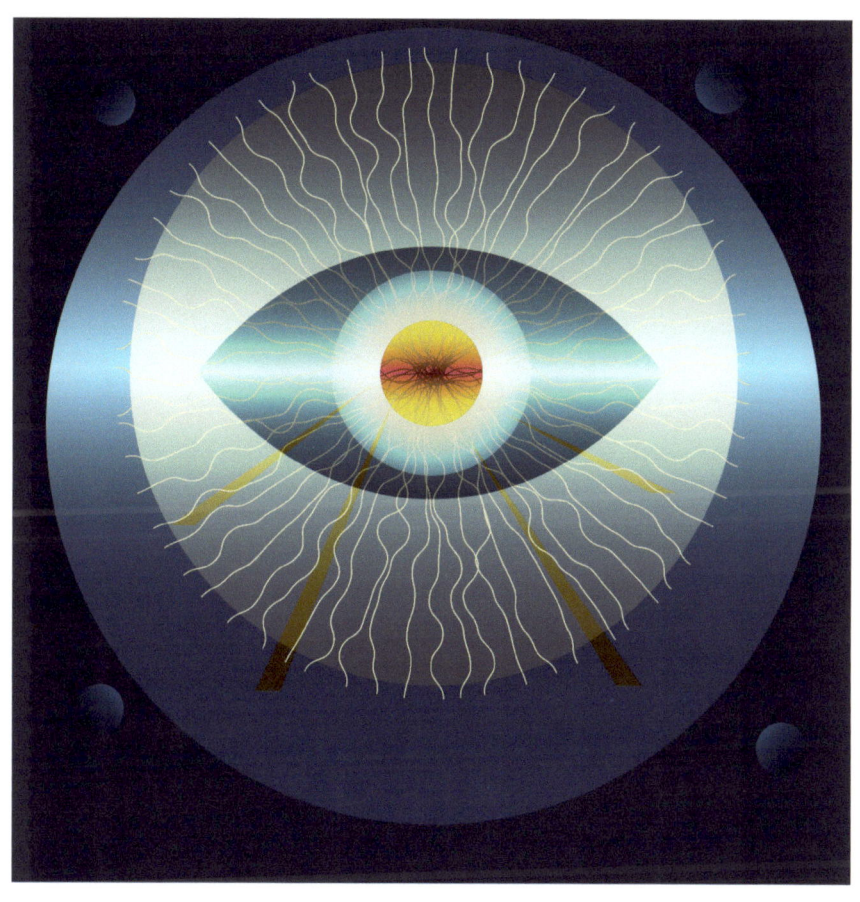

And thus begins a cycle of Creation.

#3: The Dark Bosom

There is formidable darkness from which evolution seems to have emerged. In a Cosmology of Light, and as per the ruminations of the previous post, Light as Creator, this seems paradoxical. But in fact, it becomes possible if one were to consider Light projecting itself at speed zero.

If Light were to project itself at zero speed, then the reality so created would be the opposite from that where light exists at infinite speed. This would be true because light unable to move would not be able to fill up any volume within which it existed, and hence would be the seed of extreme fragmentation, in contrast to the omnipresence in its native state.

Further, since a volume, regardless of how small or large, would not now be connected by light, there would be no way in which happenings, appearings, disappearings, could be recorded and light would be completely ignorant of anything happening in that volume, in contrast to the omniscience that would exist in its native state where it traveled infinitely fast.

If anything not of the nature of light were to arise in a volume, it would be unopposed and would freely be able to exercise its will no matter how perverse, and therefore the light would be extremely weak. This again would be in contrast to the omnipotence with which it exists in its native state.

Finally, nothing in the volume would be connected, as all is connected in light's native state, and hence there would be extreme disarray and the deliberate exercising of bad will, in contrast to harmony.

This reality, hence, would be a *Dark Bosom*, emptied completely of all the possibilities that existed in light's native state.

There are ancient traditions that refer to the creation of absolute darkness in other terms. In a Chaldean legend the powers in an original reality, of omnipresence, omnipotence, omniscience, omniharmony, confident in themselves, separated themselves from Source. As they traveled further and further, and their connection to their origin grew weaker and weaker, they finally became the opposite of themselves and plunged into a state we refer to as darkness or night.

But light remains light, and even though by this mechanism of separation or projection of zero speed there is the opposite of what existed in Light's native state, yet all of what Light is remains pregnant in each separated point, and in that aggregated and occult state of Night.

The dark bosom, hence, even though it engenders weakness, fragmentation, ignorance, strife, darkness, disarray, has somewhere within it all that Light is.

Why Light may project itself in such ways will be explored subsequently.

#4: The Titan Reign

The Dark Bosom, containing all that Light is in a mysterious, unthinkable, unknowable, and absolutely opposite form to **Light as Creator**, thereby perhaps creates the basis of the opposite notions of Heaven and Hell, or perhaps the states of a first "nothingness" where all is undifferentiated in Light and a second "nothingness" where all is undifferentiated in Darkness.

But the Darkness is created by the four powers in Light separating themselves from Source and progressively becoming the opposite of all that they were. Hence in the Darkness are the remnants or inconceivable transmutations of those powers, now powerful in another way, because they are kings in darkness.

These kings are the sons of darkness, veritable Titans that hold sway over everything that begins to or tries to emerge from that Bosom. They rule that darkness, and they rule even in worlds emergent from darkness, in any world where darkness can enter.

Hence are imposed utter fragmentation, weakness, strife, decay, ignorance, and all else that will continue to divide and keep small, so that the Titans can amass greater and greater power through exercising fear, aggression, and deceit. Kingdoms built from utter forgetfulness of light orbit around these Titans, held in their power, unendingly.

…Unless something of Light were to descend from its native plain or to emerge from the apparent darkness…

#5: Forbidden Love

The **Titans** exercise their reign in a world that has arisen from the **Dark Bosom**. But the big secret hidden in their hearts and in the heart of the dark bosom itself is that even the utter darkness is only because of the mechanics of light. Light is fully present, though apparently completely absent.

The property of knowledge in **Light's** native state, having emptied itself of that which we call knowledge, still has some essence of the thing that was knowledge, in itself, and still becomes the basis of a different genre of unique seeds that seed Space.

Time, though fragmented to the limit, and hardly able to be the means of a cohesive power by which that which is hidden in the seed can express itself, still has power however different from that in Light's native state, and still causes the perverse kernel to grow and exercise itself.

Energy works differently, without the majesty of its transformative dynamics, to still change the dark kernel into an expression of solidified darkness.

And gravity still works, albeit to build webs of destructive relationship.

And because the essence of the four was one in Light in its native state, still there is something of *that* dynamic for the belittled, darkened incarnation of fourfoldness. The first cohesive manifestation — space-time-energy-gravity — architected by the urge of oneness in light's innate properties to uphold unified fourfoldness of knowledge-power-presence-harmony, is in essence nothing other than act of love.

Such love, however, a contradiction of the very nature of the dark bosom and its titan kings, is a manifestation of *forbidden love*.

And so in spite of the darkness, and in spite of the powerful titan, something that is not of that nature initiates unendingly a signature of Forbidden Love…

#6: Titan Matter

Forbidden Love suggests that in spite of all having arisen from a bosom of darkness and controlled by the titan sons of darkness, something of the original mystery of Light seeks something of its truth by binding progressive emergences into a whole. This act is a manifestation of *Love* and happens in spite of the medium and nature of manifest existence.

Space-time-energy-gravity, as an initial emergence reflecting Light's fourfold properties of knowledge-power-presence-harmony, becomes a container initiating a signature of Love. And then in spite of itself, from the dark bosom emerge other fourfold emergences reinforcing, again and again, the mystery of love.

A cosmic fourfold electro-magnetic-wavearchetype-masspotential field emerges within space-time-energy-gravity, and light having emerged from light, induces the further fourfold emergence of quark-lepton-boson-HiggsBoson particles. Quantum particles, hence, that may appear to exist independently, still follow the law of love, and in binding together allow the emergence of a plethora of s_Shell-p_Shell-d_Shell-f_Shell atoms that themselves are an arrangement of different combinations of quantum particles.

These layers, in spite of the bosom from which they have emerged, act together to create matter. The persistent dynamics of space-time-energy-gravity, the electro-magnetic-wavearchetype-masspotential field, and material accumulations in quark-lepton-boson-Higgsboson particles from which more complex s_Shell-p_Shell-d_Shell-f_Shell atoms emerge, create matter.

But the nature of this matter is different — it is *Titan Matter*. It has emerged from darkness in spite of the darkness. Even the vast number of suns, perhaps the pinnacle of such matter, that come into being due to the underlying dynamics of space-time-energy-gravity working on matter, create a light that is of a different quality than original light.

And that is why this matter is titan matter.

#7: The Dark Pralaya

Light in its **native state** has majesty to it. All possibility is contained within it. But when this light projects itself at **zero speed** all that majesty, infinity, and fruitful potentiality are through an act of magic made to disappear and the opposite of what IS, in some now hidden realm, expresses itself instead as a dark bosom.

It is from this dark bosom that material manifestation starts. The four powers in Light become **four Titans** who now exercise control over this dark realm. But because there is still the deep and mysterious essence of light in the complete darkness, its four powers exercise themselves, in spite of the titans, and *matter* is created.

This matter is created in an initial fourfold container of space-time-energy-gravity, itself an offspring of the dark bosom and implicit fourfoldness of light. A cosmic fourfold electro-magnetic-wavearchetype-masspotential field emerges within space-time-energy-gravity, and light having emerged from light, induces the further fourfold emergence of quark-lepton-boson-HiggsBoson particles. Quantum particles, hence, that may appear to exist independently, still follow the law of **forbidden love**, and in binding together allow the emergence of a plethora of s_Shell-p_Shell-d_Shell-f_Shell atoms that themselves are an arrangement of different combinations of quantum particles.

This matter however is **titan matter**. It is made from a marriage of encompassing darkness being infiltrated by light. And this titan matter creates titan suns that express a dark light. There is no emergence as yet of an organizing principle that would be strong enough to withstand the gravitational pull of darkness. And this manifestation, this dark bosom, seeing the emergence of titan matter and titan suns in spite of the infinity of its darkness, functions as a massive black hole to pull back all manifested into the darkness.

This pullback of titan matter and titan suns into the dark bosom can be thought of as *The Dark Pralaya*.

#8: Hidden Knowledge

In the mythology that arises from a cosmology of light, Light is the creator of the cosmos. In this act of creation, the conditions chosen as the starting point of the cosmic adventure are set by light projecting itself at speed zero, which ensures a dark bosom, reign of the titans, love that is forbidden, matter fashioned by the strange union of what is in light emerging in vast hostility, inevitably leading to substantial instability as suggested by the dark pralaya.

And such an outcome would be a forever recurring cycle if it were not for the dynamics of a manifestation preceding a pralaya somehow changing the nature of the dark bosom itself.

While time may be reset each time dissolution into the dark vast occurs, yet somewhere else "time" proceeds differently so that unexpressed potentiality hid deep in light might express itself in completely different forms of matter.

There is a *hidden knowledge* that builds up in the dark bosom, a knowledge that compels more of an opening as it were to the ever-existent light, and the next emergence becomes different because of this.

Something in the dark bosom is allowed to change with the cosmic adventure that has sunk back into it so that subsequent adventures and pralayas are hence different, as a result of that.

#9: The Last Pralaya

Light arises in spite of darkness, and perhaps simply because darkness is a stance of light.

But the nature of the darkness can be overwhelming. Then even the matter that arises in acts of forbidden love has a nature such that it yields ultimately to the darkness.

But if the darkness begins to change its very nature so that it fundamentally tends more and more to the nature of light, then the matter created may not yield eventually to darkness. But that already suggests that the phenomenon of pralaya is over.

Legend suggests that six pralayas have occurred, and the current creation, the seventh, will not yield to darkness. But it is only through hidden knowledge being built up in the darkness that darkness ultimately allows that which stands behind it to become more ingrained in its substance.

Such manifestation means that the forms being manifested inherently want to choose light over darkness at the margin — in the small acts that occur in time.

But in the *Last Pralaya* — the one that as legend suggests preceded this creation — manifested matter must have been subject to a struggle between light and darkness such that light often got the upper hand, but eventually did yield to the darkness…

…Though not before the Hidden Knowledge had reached such a stage that the perpetual victory of light was close…

Part 2: Mysteries of Light

#10: The Secret of c

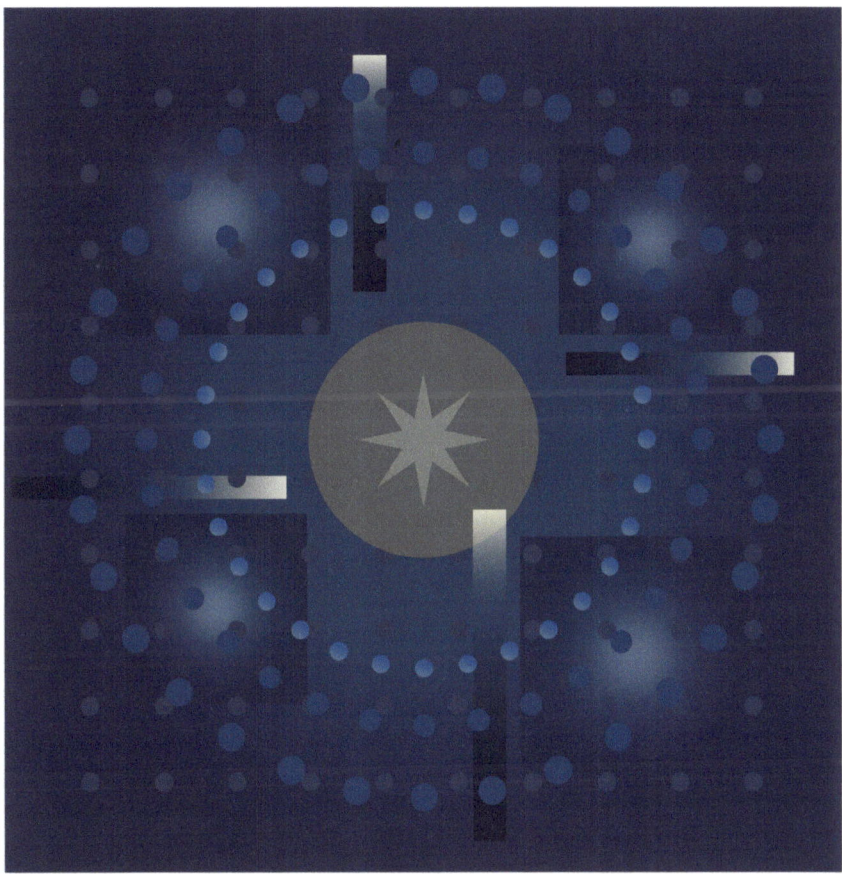

From somewhere within the **native state of Light**, where it travels infinitely fast and its substance is omnipotent, omniscient, omnipresent, and omniharmonious, Light looks out and sees and hears all that is.

It sees and hears how the call from the layer of reality engendered by Light being projected at speed zero is changing its nature. Through the **series of pralayas**, something of the experience of the dissolved manifestation settles into its substance creating a **hidden knowledge**. This knowledge changes the nature of the fundamental cry emanating from matter itself because that which could have been but was not, yearns more to be.

It does not even know what it wants to be, but that stance, that build-up of the fundamental urge that cannot even know exactly what it desires, passes a threshold and seeing that the ensuing balance in a subsequent manifestation can be different, that Light which sees and hears all, allows a different dynamic to enter into the creation of the next cosmos.

Light from the core, from its native state, prepares a different and multifaceted descent, and substantial to this descent is the projection also of Light at the speed c - 186,000 miles per second in vacuum. The projection at speed c allows a different possibility for matter- thus far continually incarnated as **Titan Matter** - to become something different, so that matter might progressively unveil more of all that is in Light itself.

This is the wonder, this the possibility, this the secret.

For, the physics of light projected at c is such that the very basis of matter can change. The harmony of its speed allows information in Light to express itself in a different material way, and such that the possibilities of such matter opening to more and more light will be increased.

In the multifacetedness of the descent, something more of the *core* of Light is *central,* and that Light anchoring itself in light projected at zero and light projected at c, can orchestrate an adventure that allows a pralaya never to occur again. Never again need material manifestation harried and ultimately overcome by its own titan dysfunction, seek refuge in a return to the dark bosom.

Forever are changed the dynamics of cosmos, so that now the previously central figures of the dark bosom, the **titans**, and the reality of titan matter, have to contend with *Her* — something or someone deep within or even hidden by Light's core — and the possibilities of the instrumentation she has bought into being, manifest through matter that will be created by light traveling at speed c, and other descents of light yet to be spoken about.

#11: c-World Embryo

Light at c allows another world to be created. This world is relative to the native world of light. This, in contrast to light projected at zero, which is an absolute other. The world created from light at c is a closer relative to the native world of light, allowing therefore, more of the infinity in light to manifest…

This *c-World* creates a stable substance, a foundation, that allows another kind of matter to form in it, in another way. Titan matter emerged in spite of its context, because of the love that is forbidden in the world where there is no light. c-World is created because light slows down to a degree that allows that which is hidden in light to show itself in another way. Love is no longer forbidden and light acts openly.

There is differentiation of the infinity held previously as oneness, and as vast number of subtle seeds borne by *light-love* express themselves in first material form, a big bang is precipitated.

This big bang or crack is the first womb of material creation ushering in first substance into a c-World embryo…birth in light will now beget birth of light…

#12: The Birth of Space-Time-Energy-Gravity

The creation of the **c-World embryo** has many secrets hidden in it.

The first is that its overt dynamics are managed by the macro-entity Space-Time-Energy-Gravity. Some perhaps would call her a god.

For in this **new descent** culminating in light establishing itself as speed c, other resting places, other embryos, other dynamics were established. At each place in this journey, light showed itself in another way. The subtlety and oneness opened its heart more, and something different, from its inner substance, stepped forth. Older gods with precise purposes were born of these other embryos, to assist their younger sister, space-time-energy-gravity with her task of molding emergence in the c-World embryo.

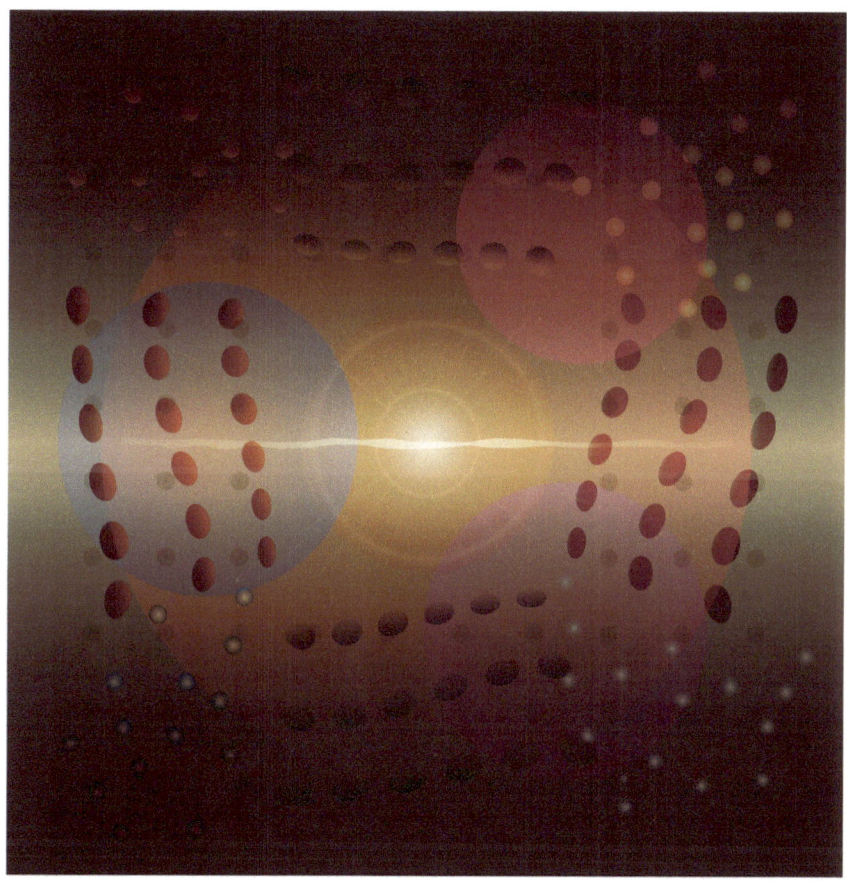

For when light arrived at c, the crack, the big bang, let forth an infinity of seeds, that would forever be held together in a fateful embrace by space-time-energy-gravity, where Space is the arena where infinite seeds will express themselves, Time will allow the secret in each seed to mature, Energy will allow the subtle in the seed to become material, and Gravity will allow seed to cohort with seed in relationships pregnant with meaning.

#13: The Ever-Present Priest

c-World embryo has many secrets hidden in it. A goddess, born from light, who manages its macro-dynamics is **space-time-energy-gravity**. She came into being with the **fateful descent of light** to speed c and holds in her embrace potentiality seeking to materialize more of the infinity in Light.

But the cosmos is living, and at every moment the dynamics due to many beings, **titan influences**, gods and goddesses, mingle, and something from the mix determines the incremental steps that will forever alter space-time-energy-gravity.

And this great arbitration is presided over by the ever-present priest, born as twin to his larger sister, space-time-energy-gravity. For this priest is nothing other than of the substance of space-time-energy-gravity. The unfolding of each seed, or being, requires his blessing to change the active space-time-energy-gravity code that defines the way and possibility of that being.

In each moment a being may actively tap into the deeper dynamics antecedent in other layers of light, stay in the groove prescribed by the space-time-energy-gravity code already in place, or even open to titan influences emanating from that layer where light has been projected at zero speed.

And this active dynamic will evoke a different response from the ever-present space-time-energy-gravity priest. If he remains untouched, then space-time-energy-gravity law for that being remains the same or even alters based on titan influence. But if he is moved, he may carry the fire to the antecedent planes, enticing the dynamics there to descend into a new incarnation of the being's specific space-time-energy-gravity law.

Then more of the fourfoldness hidden in light materializes and the cosmos steps into even greater aliveness.

#14: The Edge of Light

There is magic in a face appearing amidst the apparent emptiness. All are drawn to it and get transfixed by it. All becomes subject to it and see only in reference to it. The edge of light is just such a magician.

For having appeared in its form of apparent electromagnetism, Light is seen only as it. But this is only an illusion. Light is forever multi-dimensional replete with infinite possibility in its deepest folds — the greatest of all magicians.

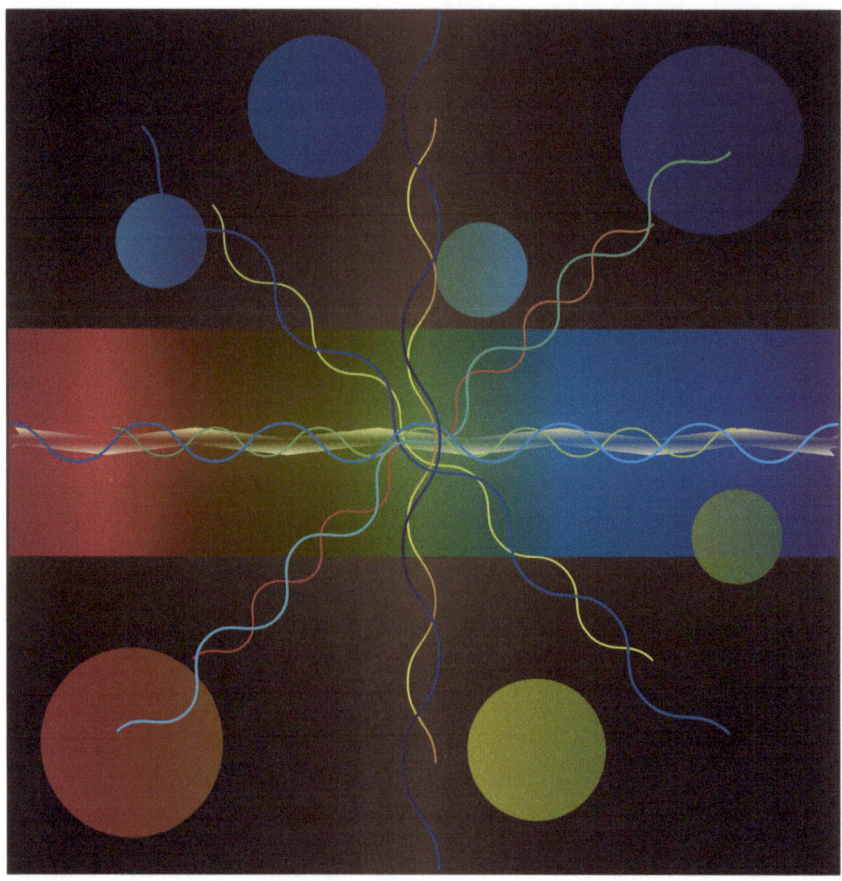

The first veil is that the fourfoldness of light gets hidden by its aspects of power and harmony. The 'electro' hints at the 'power' aspect of light, which varies as the frequency of light varies. The 'magnetic' hints at the 'harmony' aspect of light. But also there is the 'knowledge' aspect apparent by the range of wavelengths that light consists of, and the 'presence' aspect' at the base of different kinds of masses or forms of matter that will arise based on frequency of light.

This magical embodiment, traveling at c, sets up some means and pathways that will remain central to future surfacings in c-World Embryo. But this is only an edge of all else that will come forward, compelled by the nature of what it really is…

#15: The Crucible of Love

The Secret of c alluded to *Her*: that powerful core hidden by Light. That of which all Light in all its form is but an instrument. When She looked out at the troubled manifestation as it journeyed through pralayas to reach the last pralaya, She sent forth something of herself that was remarkable.

This special descent of Love, embodying openly a love so different than the forbidden love that worked in the dark bosom against the titan reign, was accompanied by light traveling at c and by various gods arranged as meta-function in antecedent layers of light.

This Love, a flame of Her being, called into existence different arrangements of Light's fourfoldness. **Space-time-energy-gravity** appeared magically through the crack we call the big bang, and we met the ever-p[resent priest of the sacrifice, ready to take high-flaming aspiration, sincerity, purity, and other siblings born from the ardor of the human travail to ancestral gods resident in antecedent layers.

These central fourfold beings, and all those that are yet to arise, are formidable only because their fourfoldness is held together by this Love. This Love that is so powerful, this Love that is the secret of Light, this Love that maintains that explicit integrality of form to reflect the implicit nature of that which is hidden in Light. This Love, which shall yet prove to be the crucible in which Light in all its glory will step forth…

#16: The First of the Multiverse Mysteries

There are many preparations required before light in all its glory can step forth from the crucible of love. The edge of light is only an early child whose nature is to spread itself rapidly within the space-time-energy-gravity container. In so doing it enables pathways to be used by future creations.

But many future creations require magic similar to the creation of the macro space-time-energy-gravity container, to be set up on a microscale. Gods and goddesses from antecedent planes of light have to lend something of themselves in a union to create these micro-entities.

What results is a first slew of quantum particles. For the edge of light is coaxed into lending its wave-like form to settle into god-enabled knowledge-based, power-based, harmony-based, and presence-based material accumulations, forming a multiverse of quarks, leptons, bosons, and Higgs-bosons respectively.

These first subtle wave-particle dualities reproduce themselves endlessly creating copies that have all the antecedent power of light and its dynamics behind or in them. Hence, they are the first multiverses: complete wholenesses that resemble one another, parallel creations, therefore, that yet live in the same space-time-energy-gravity container.

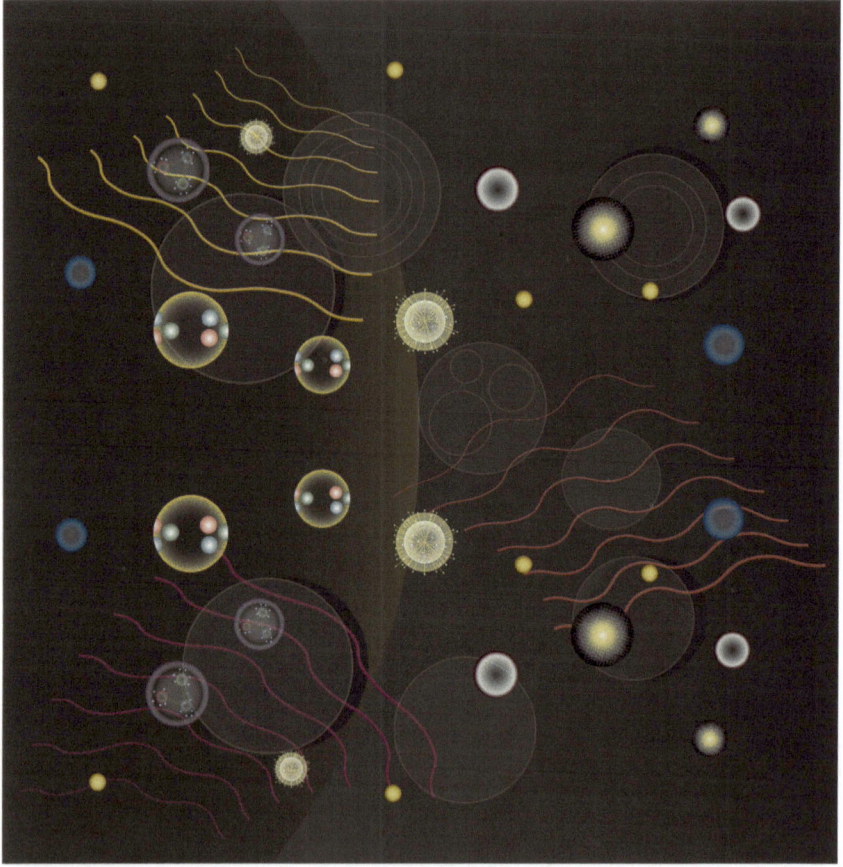

This is the first multiverse mystery that is barely considered. Understanding this lends a new appreciation for Cosmos.

#17: The Wonder of Atomic-Equilibria

Shepherded by the four invisible presences the multiverse of quantum particles is shaped into the holy chain of 108 atoms. Each atom embodies a unique meta-function instrumental to the play of possibility in the macro space-time-energy-gravity container.

There is the category of atoms of power such as hydrogen and helium. The great adventurers whose consciousness sets up the broad dynamics of atomic possibility, allowing other categories of atoms to manifest in star-containers created by their fusion.

There is the category of atoms of presence such as iron and nickel. Immensely stable, these are the workhorses that bind together bigger and bigger structure through their solidness. Adventure marries concreteness to get further grounded in manifestation.

There is the category of atoms of harmony such as cerium and europium. Experimentations in collectivity, binding together a larger number of quantum particles at the atomic level.

There is the category of atoms of knowledge such as carbon and silicon. Vehicles of intelligence, they also contain archetypal possibilities that will be reflected in all other categories of atoms. Chains and conglomerates of atoms yield to their impulsion.

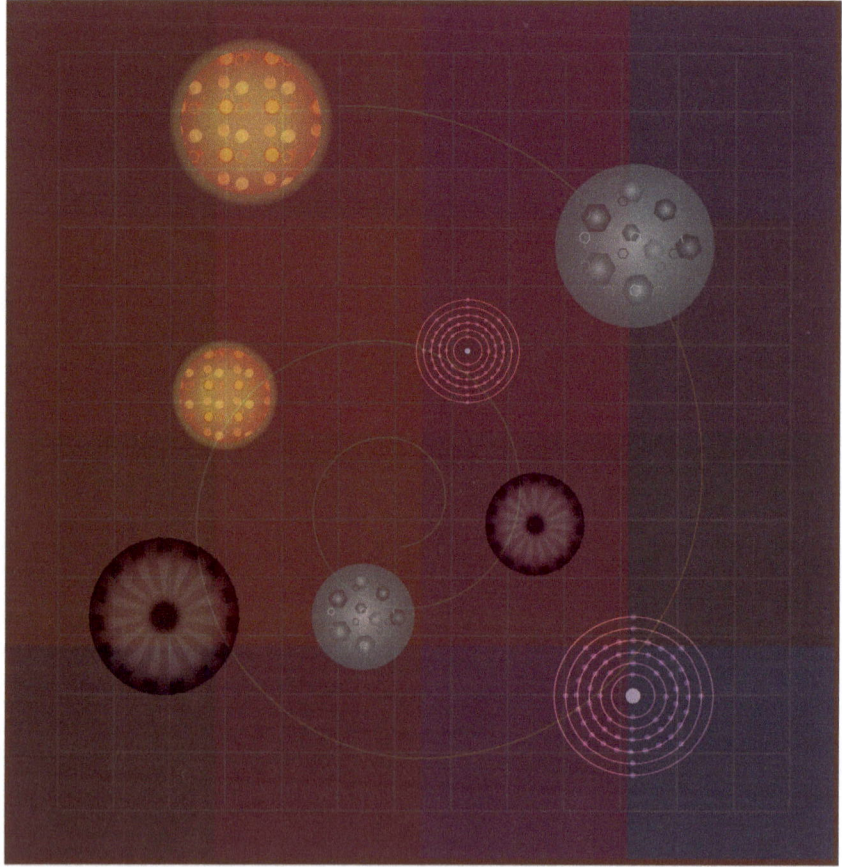

Magnificent wholenesses, bound to hold within them extraordinary force and possibility, each atom of the holy chain is not only a world onto itself, replete with the fourfold dynamics of Light, but also the foundation for all future material possibility.

To look within reveals as much mystery as the mystery that will be built outwardly through them. Veritably, a wonder of equilibrium…

#18: The Essence of Life

There is something called Life that emerges from the **crucible of love**. A powerful movement that originates in the far recesses of light, where light exists in its **native state**, it carries in it all that Light is.

But that is not all. It is the dynamic width, height, breadth, the veritable volume within which all that Light is will express itself.

We have met already primary currents in its flow: the **macro space-time-energy-gravity container**, the **micro and ever-present priest**; and the significant eddies: the **edge of light** that crisscrosses across its expanse, the **mysterious quantum multiverses** that fluctuate between visibility and invisibility, and the first **formidable equilibria** between inner and outer housed in the bodies of atoms, that constitute its growing body.

Each of these expresses something fundamental of light's fourfoldness. With each step, the implicit infinity in Light materializes as explicit wonder, continuing to be bound together, or rather driven, by the perpetual presence of love. With each step, something more of what is hidden, something more of what is meant by the fourfold properties of presence, power, knowledge, and harmony, comes forward. With each step variation increases. With each step, it becomes abundantly apparent that infinity is showing itself.

This then is the essence of Life — the mystery of infinite light forever expressing itself in ever-more complete, ever-more dynamic manifestations of love….

#19: The Miracle of the Cell

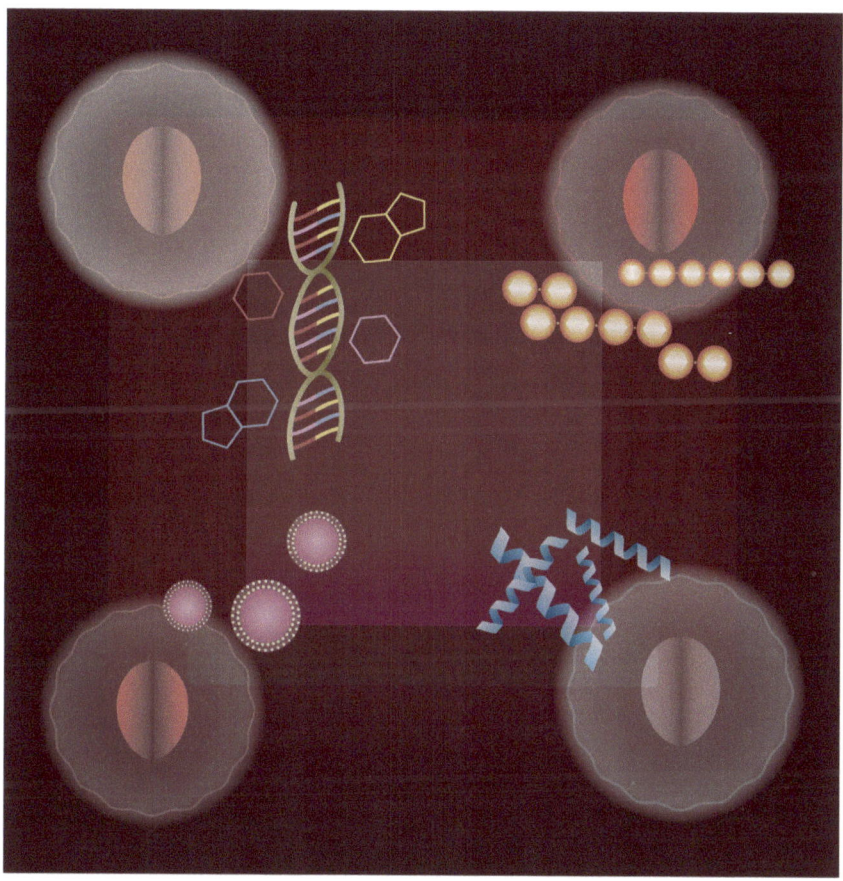

As **Life advances** more complex forms have to manifest to keep step with its pace. **Atoms** already housed fathomless power in them, and through the wonder of combination continue to give rise to an infinite number of molecules.

And then these molecules, containing **universes** in themselves, under the aegis of the guiding Light are compelled to combine together in master formulae to give rise to four foundational plans complete enough to hold the ever-more intricate rhythms central to the evolution of Life.

We call these foundational plans Nucleic Acids, Polysaccharides, Proteins, and Lipids, and each is a special vehicle for Light, grounding a more advanced iteration of Light's fourfoldness — knowledge, power, presence, and harmony — respectively.

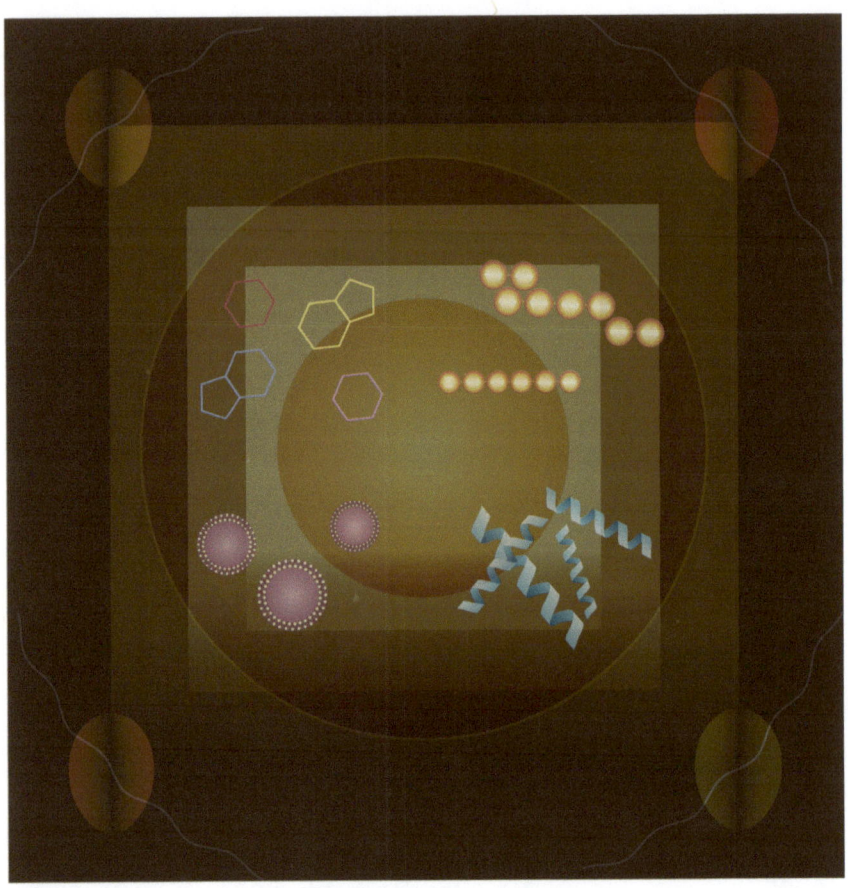

The goddesses of knowledge tie together four mysterious blocks in strands capable of being the basis of infinite information, the goddesses of power create wells of energy capable of sustaining life in its vicinity, the goddesses of presence multiply function as form to create all manner of minute device, and the goddesses of harmony manifest wise division to allow work to specialize and coordinate.

And when these four master-creations are held together by Love, there arises a veritable miracle — a world so complete, inhabited by millions of beings, forming the basis of all that is yet come — the Cell!

Part 3: The Making of History

#20: The Inevitable Battle

When the **cell emerged** all the universes paused to wonder at the miracle. Layers of light — and the gods and goddesses presiding over these — had been attendant in its birth. Something of their being had participated in it. Something of their substance had been imparted into it.

Trillions of **quantum-level multiverses** dancing on an **edge of light**, and billions of **atom-based equilibria** chanting an endless and creative ode of 108-fold joy, participated in creating the fourfold molecular pathways that would embody a massive advance in a **leap of Life**.

The **ever-present priest** sat in ubiquitous trance within the bosom of his larger **space-time-energy-gravity sister**, aware that with the birth of the cell his raison d'etre was about to be tested, and his activity about to be raised a million-fold.

For this master foundation of all that was about to emerge, was not only the object of wonder of all manner of light-filled beings but also the sought-for prize of the **titans of the dark**. For whoever exercised their reign in this cellular world arisen from miracle, would apparently become the master of **fourfoldness**.

The light-beings sought for a continued play of fourfoldness which would invite greater and greater forms for them to not only incarnate into but perhaps even to continue to grow in. The titans of the dark, on the other hand, sought control of fourfoldness and the spreading of fear and its attendant poisons of darkness in its wake. This would allow them to live — even undetected — and stamp their restricting influence in all living things.

The scene, hence, was set for an inevitable battle.

#21: The Vanity of the Strangle-Hold

Dumb-founded by the continual descents of light apparent in the ever-more resplendent architectures of fourfoldness, and hungry to exercise their grip, just as they had in ages-old when titan-matter was the norm, the sons of darkness surfaced with force to gain control of the miracle of the cell.

Their means and ways had remained intact in their bosom or origin, and they effectively mobilized these to seep into the dynamics of the cell. Little did they realize how strategic a victory this would be. For, all manner of cell-based life — plants and animals and humans and various other peoples across the universe whose foundation was this master-emergence — were yet to surface.

Their victory would lock cell-based creation into a stranglehold so severe that for eons life would be stunted, essentially accustomed to perceiving only darkness and on rare occasion noticing light. This was the ultimate and ever-present paradox — having emerged from light, being of the nature of light, surrounded by and filled with light, life yet would be overwhelmingly blind to it.

Because of this stranglehold, doubt and fear and anger and anxiety, amongst a hundred other restricting movements, would be alive to maintain darkness and smallness and keep the light from becoming aware of itself.

But such awareness is inevitable.

The secret of c, the c-World embryo, the birth of space-time-energy-gravity, the ever-present priest, amongst other antecedent light-based deities who all accompanied Her in the descent, would assure the vanity of the stranglehold…

#22: The Gift

The **stranglehold**, even though vain, is real.

Because of it, the wonder of the trillions of **quantum-level multiverses** dancing on an **edge of light** will be lost. Because of it, the chant of the billions of **atom-based equilibria** seeking to express their 108-fold joy will remain but a murmur. Because of it, the creativity of the fourfold molecular pathways seeking to embody **leaps of life** will remain stunted.

That which could have been, will not be now, but only after the **battle** has been waged, and only after the ever-present **priest** has traveled into the depths of the bosom of his **space-time-energy-gravity sister** a million times, delivering fire to the antecedent gods and goddesses, until they become convinced that life truly wants to embody light.

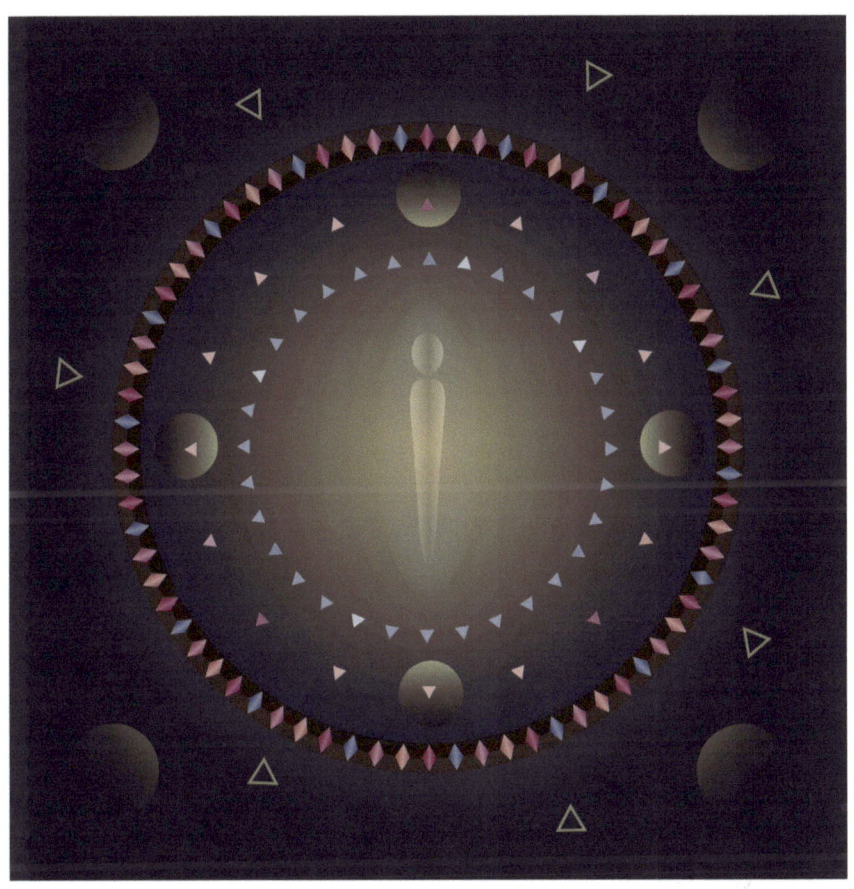

That after all is the gift of the terrible stranglehold, itself conceived in the deepest layers of light where all is held together in a prophetic and propitious embrace.

Matter and life have to endure, to grow, so that a billion diamond faces can fully express overwhelming beauty in every play in time and space.

#23: Pioneers of Light

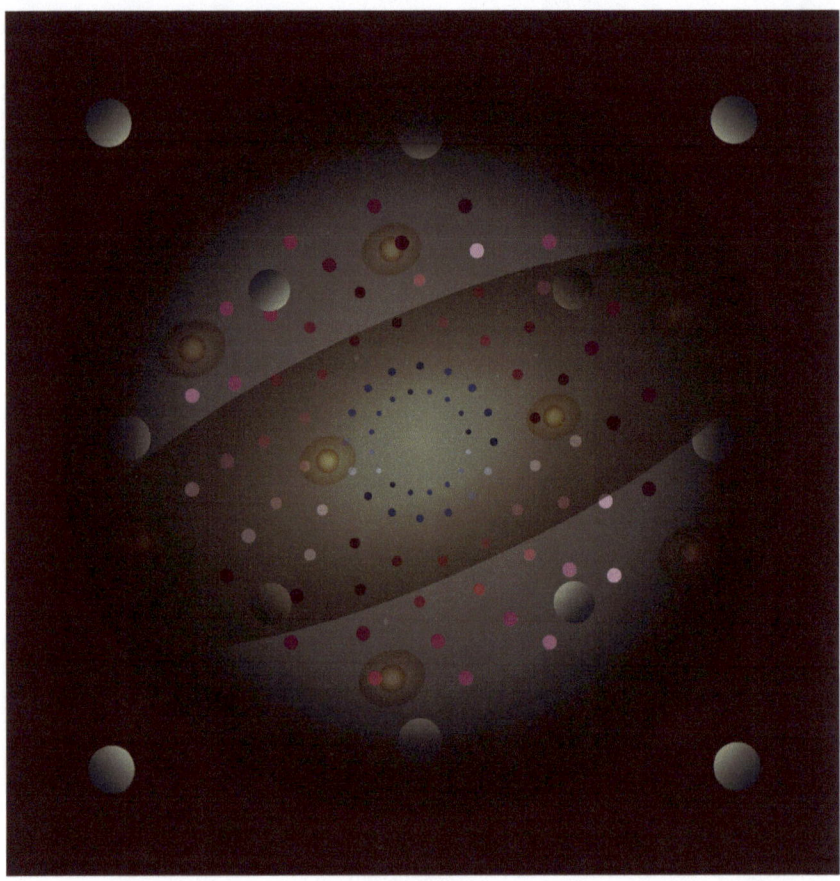

The **titan stranglehold** effectively placed a lid on the myriad creations, possibilities, and wonders of light. Light and its infinite potentiality — of which **quantum particles**, **atoms**, molecules, and **cells** are only partial emergences — remained hidden.

Life, playing itself out in billions of cell-based creations, essentially remained oblivious of the wonders of light hidden away in the unconsidered recesses.

But when **She came**, dynamics began to change, and aspects of Her began to manifest in persons here and there. Something of Her connection, view, and command of light incarnated in pioneers, who, despite the titan-control, could pierce behind the veil and see the thousand-fold riches that existed in the minutia of manifestation.

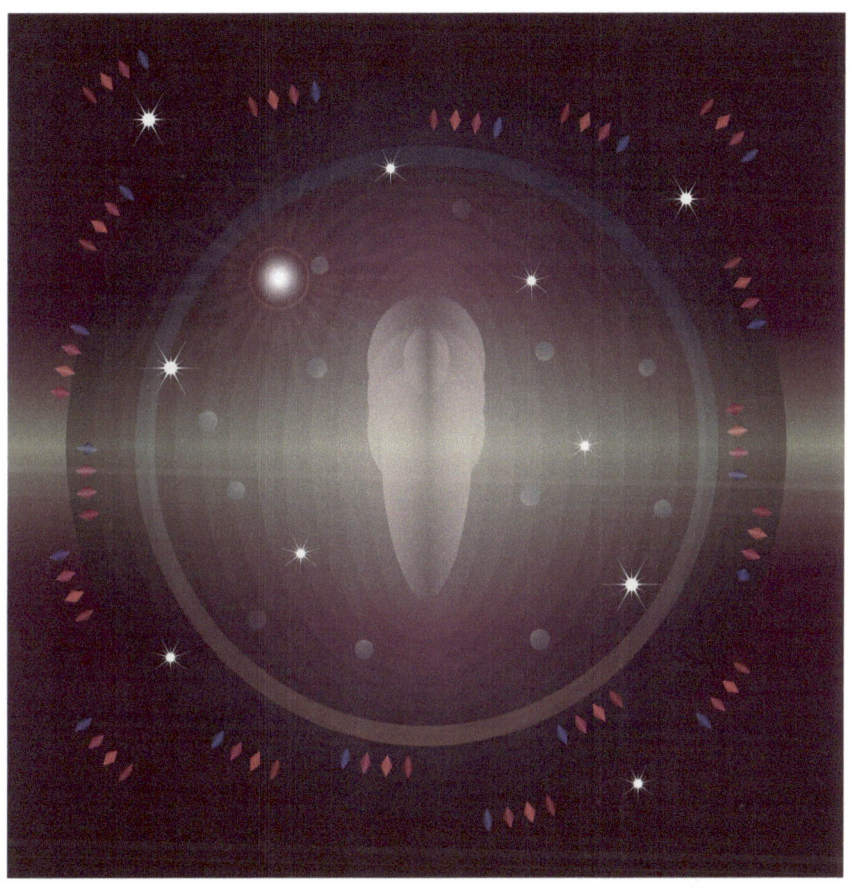

New philosophies, new legends, new mythologies, new ways of being, new possibilities, began to emerge in the material field surrounding these pioneers of light…

#24: She

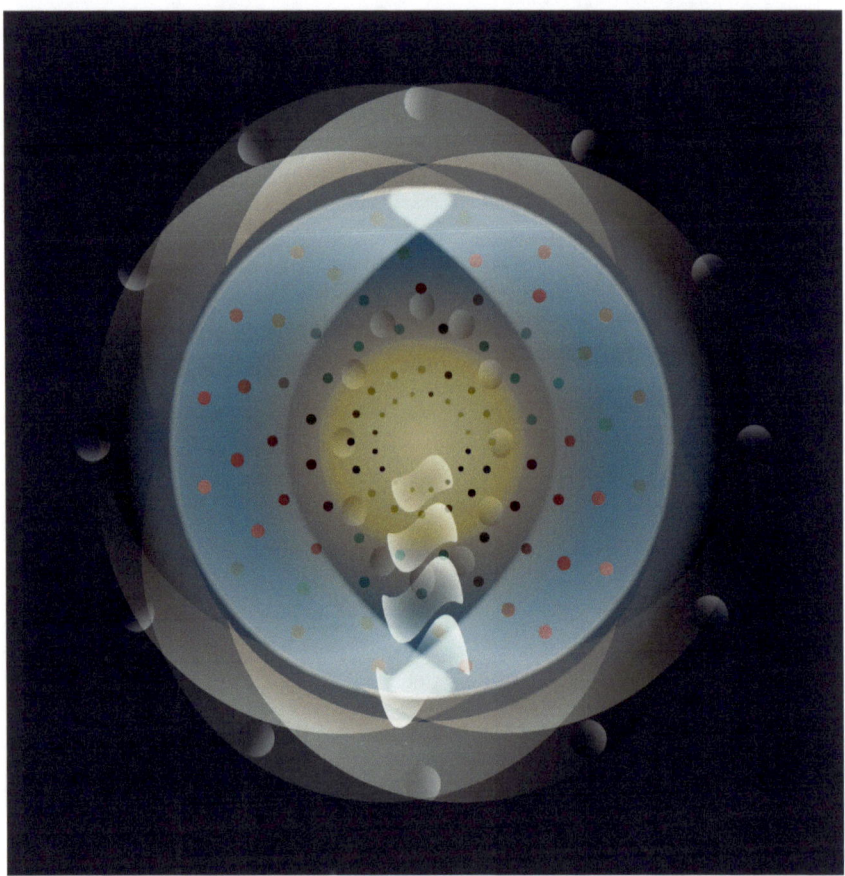

Who is She?

That Wonder, with whose descent light precipitated to c. That Mystery, who bought with her myriads of antecedent gods and goddesses, governing the deeper layers where light travels faster than c.

All Light is only an outer garment she wears to materialize more of who she is in the manifestation. That native state of Light where it travels infinitely fast is only an out-flashing from a deeper Eye, which she opened briefly, to precipitate this play.

But She, in her fullness, is behind all out-flashing Light. She meditated, and her intention went forth in the flash, becoming progressively clearer in the progressiveness of Manifestation.

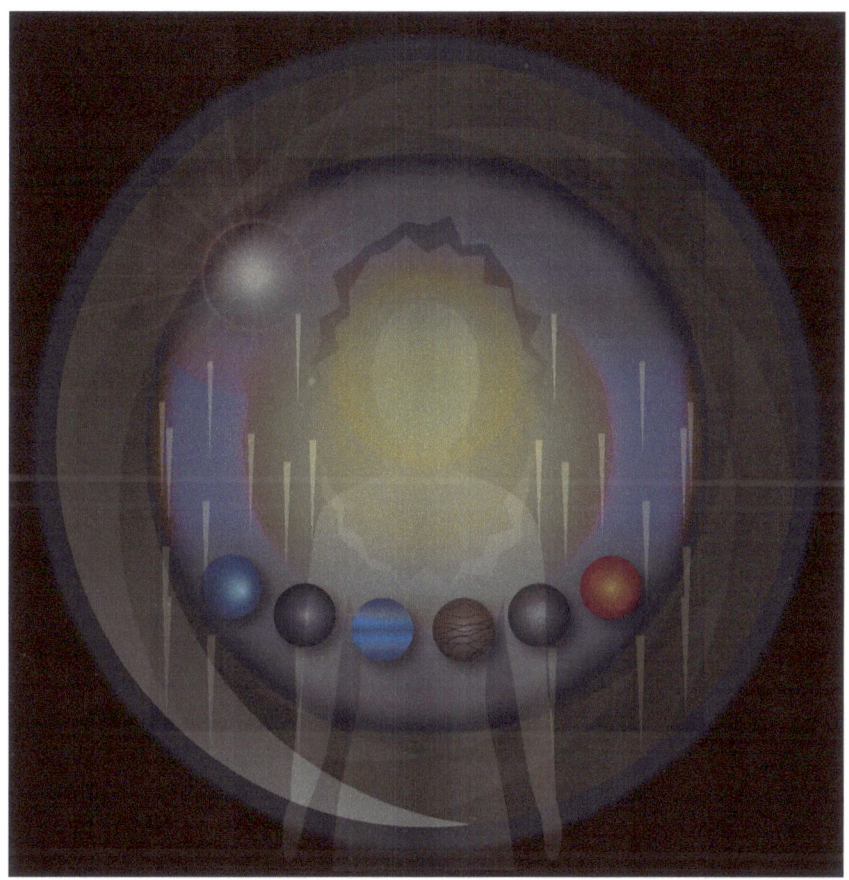

All the births of Light, the c-world embryo, space-time-energy-gravity, the ever-present priest, the edge of light, the multiverse quanta, atomic-equilibria, the cell, the pioneers, and all the wonders yet to come, are all her children, even as were the earlier mysteries of the dark bosom, the titans, forbidden love, titan matter, and the pralayas.

Verily, all is She.

#25: He

For **Her** to materialize in her fullness in the earth-play, there must be eons of preparation with ambassadors, protagonists, heroes, and massive descents of light first paving the way.

There would be no use for her to come, after all, if the earth, its inhabitants, and earth-substance itself could not receive more of that fullness. And that is why in the past, she had sent only parts of herself.

And still, she would need to be convinced that it was time for her to radically alter the slow-paced trajectory of the cosmos. Was it time to change the **balance of matter** so that the sun-born particles and atoms forever remaining open to titan influence emanating from the dark bosom, would once and for all forgo that dark alliance and step instead into new seeds and kernels faithful only to light?

For this to happen, the deeper mystery of **Oneness** present even before the initial flashing out of Light that precipitated the play of the cosmos would need to materially display more of that oneness. Her mirror-self — He — in whose stability she dances new worlds into creation, would need to bind with her in ways that have never been done before so that Oneness, as it was in the deeper mystery, can become real even here in the material manifestation.

He would need to call Her from this other end of possibility. And for that, He would himself need to have first been present here…

#26: The Destined Courtship

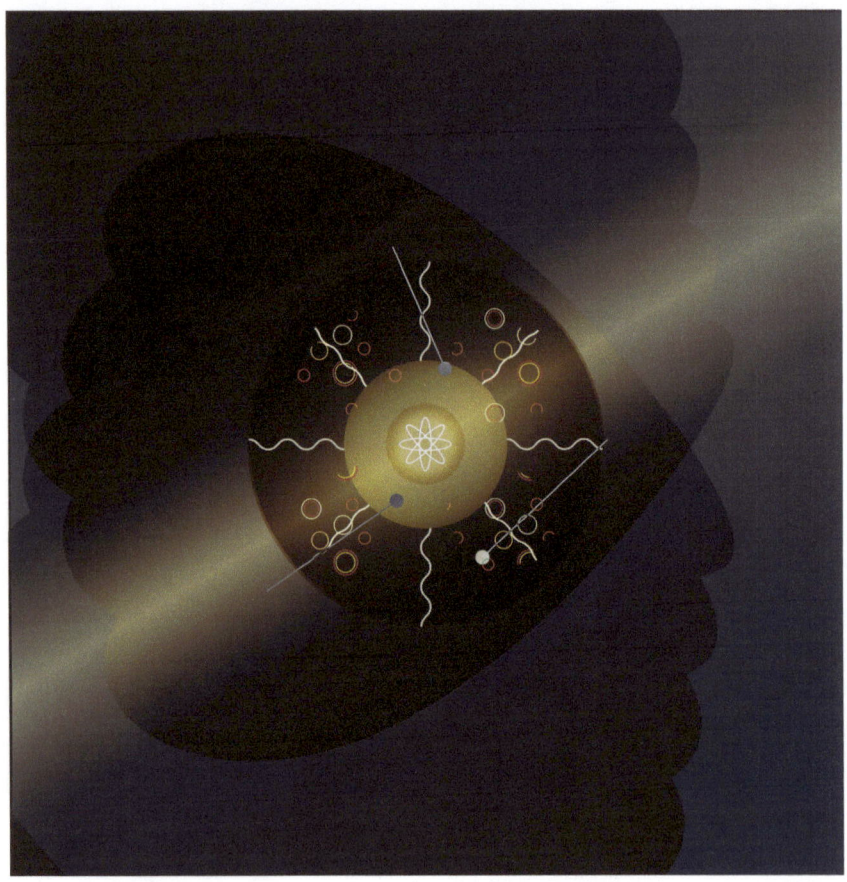

The **original flash** emanating at infinite speed and creating the first container, the first tremendous *packet* of light, in which all else — even the darkness — is going to take place, is a great act of magic.

But the greatest magical act is when **He**, from his state beyond light, projects himself at **zero speed** to engulf all light. He in which all light is imminent and free now projects himself in such a way that all light remains imminent but bound. The light cannot travel, the light cannot connect, the light cannot be the substance in which all else takes place, and therefore that which is engendered can never know.

He becomes the eternal somnambulist, darkness enveloped only by darkness. He sits, immense and alone, not just with darkness as his robe, not just within that darkness, but as the darkness itself. He who bore vast identity with Her in an original Oneness, has become now the alpha-point initiating a long journey toward an omega-point that must culminate in material Oneness where He and She are again One.

She must enter manifestation as all the layers of light until light itself forms a single edifice containing all its speeds from zero to infinity. This greatest act of magic hence, precipitates emergence and emergence, descent and descent, and the destined and long courtship between He and She.

#27: The Envisioning of Earth

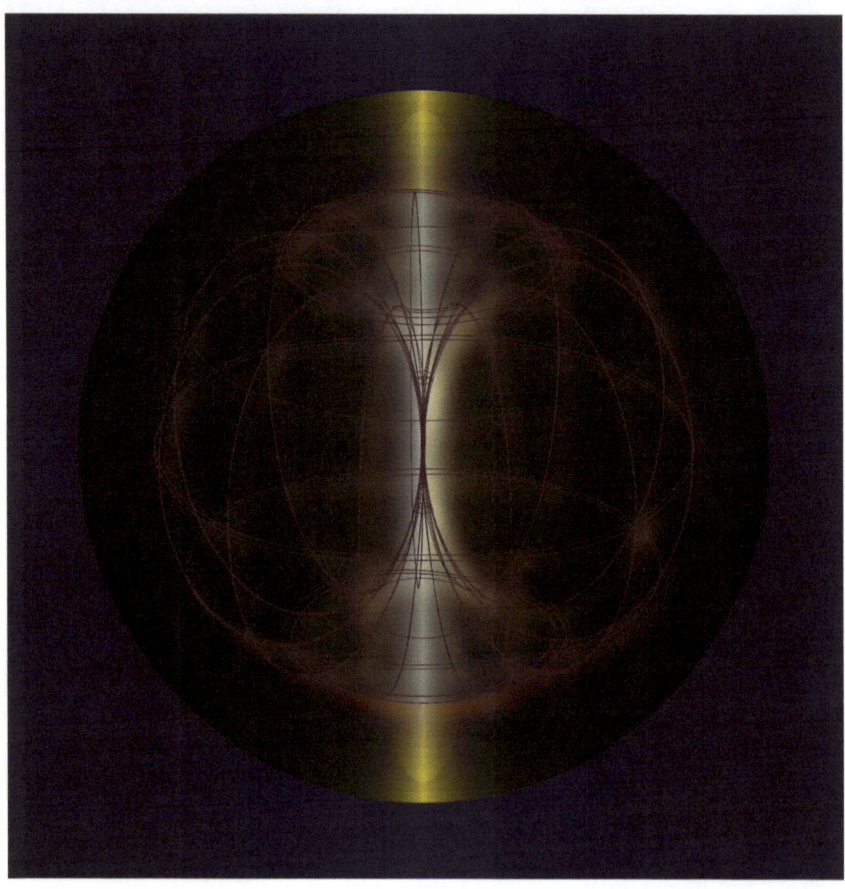

Pralayic loops are inevitable in the early stages of their **courtship**. In his somnambulist trance, he creates a universe centered around the dark bosom. Titans reign, and all matter itself is only **titan-matter**. The rays of the resulting titan-light are not strong enough to escape the gravity of the darkness and loop back into the Night.

She, called by the apparent distress of her **eternal lover**, comes, but cannot come in all her glory since that would be futile. Nothing can open to her height of power and possibility, yet. Instead, she can only send parts of herself to participate, and influence by part of her infinite capacities, to slowly shift the turmoil.

It is so that some **early pioneers** pierce something of the dark veil and see there, the hidden treasures of Light in the heart of darkness. No longer will the **multiverse quantum worlds** need to draw only from other dark worlds. Even the possibility of **cells** shifting away from the fatal influence glimmers on the horizon.

And so the memory of light grows, and with the **last pralaya**, something in Him is awake enough now, to admit a different trajectory. She seizes the opportunity, and a series of new descents begin that will create the single edifice encompassing all the speeds of light.

Her Grace, **manifest as c**, begins a new process for the formation of matter. It is no longer the stark titan-matter that inevitably ends in pralaya. Instead, there is the possibility of a mixture, formed from particles created by the higher light and particles created by the darkness.

The stage has now been set, and the adventure in c-World embryo can take a different route to change the nature of matter. But new centers of activity that will allow new intensities in their eternal courtship, first need to be created.

In the antecedent layers, the envisioning of Earth begins…

#28: Earth

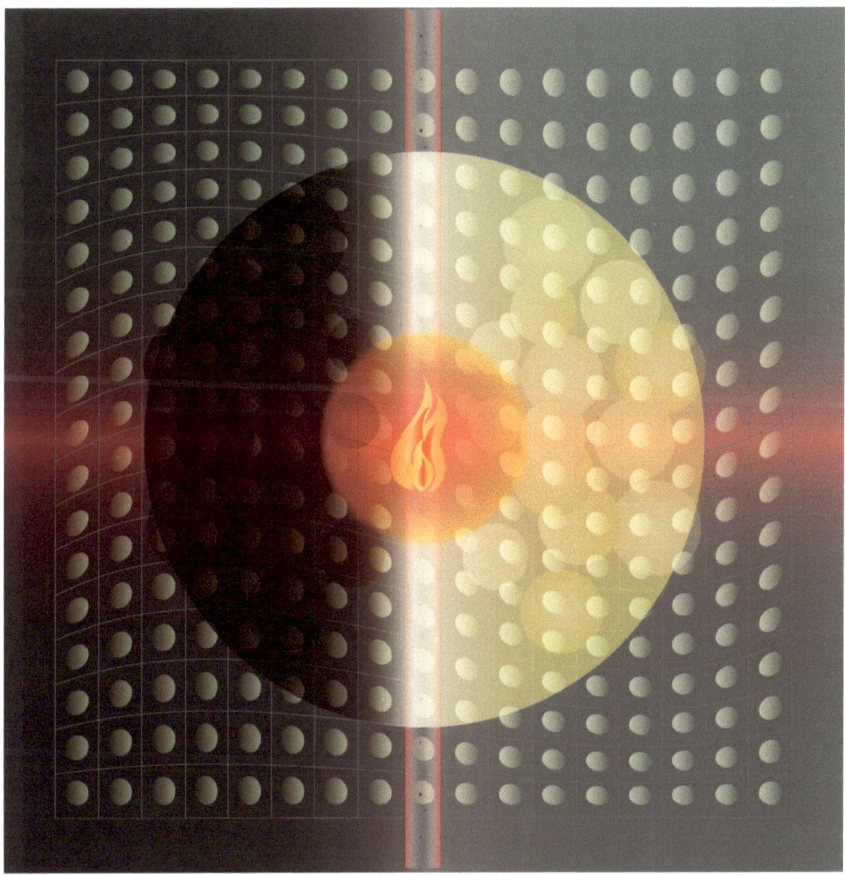

Quantum-level multiverses imply that all is deeply connected to all. Change in one place will then inevitably impact all other places — it is so that the cosmos was formed. As a result, the real work of change in matter from a base of night to light, need then only be concentrated in one place.

That place, Earth, would be the center of extraordinary activity. Not only because it would house the courtship in material form between Him and Her but also because a special descent of light, a fire, a flame, would have to be at the center of this planet for it to benefit from the massive changes made by the interaction between Him and Her. That flame would be able to hold change even whilst matter in its continued weakness was still not able to do so.

That descent of light, though, would allow Matter to become bolder, would allow it — in time — to forego the **dark titan alliance** it had become so used to. That flame, existing too in the inhabitants of Earth, would allow permanent progressive dynamics so that even when individual material sheaths were shed, the essential forward movement made by the individual would be carried by the individualized centers of light.

Earth, hence, would exist around a special flame, would house inhabitants similarly existing around individualized flames, would be the center of the **material courtship** between Him and Her, and therefore the destined place where Matter itself would change its base from night to light.

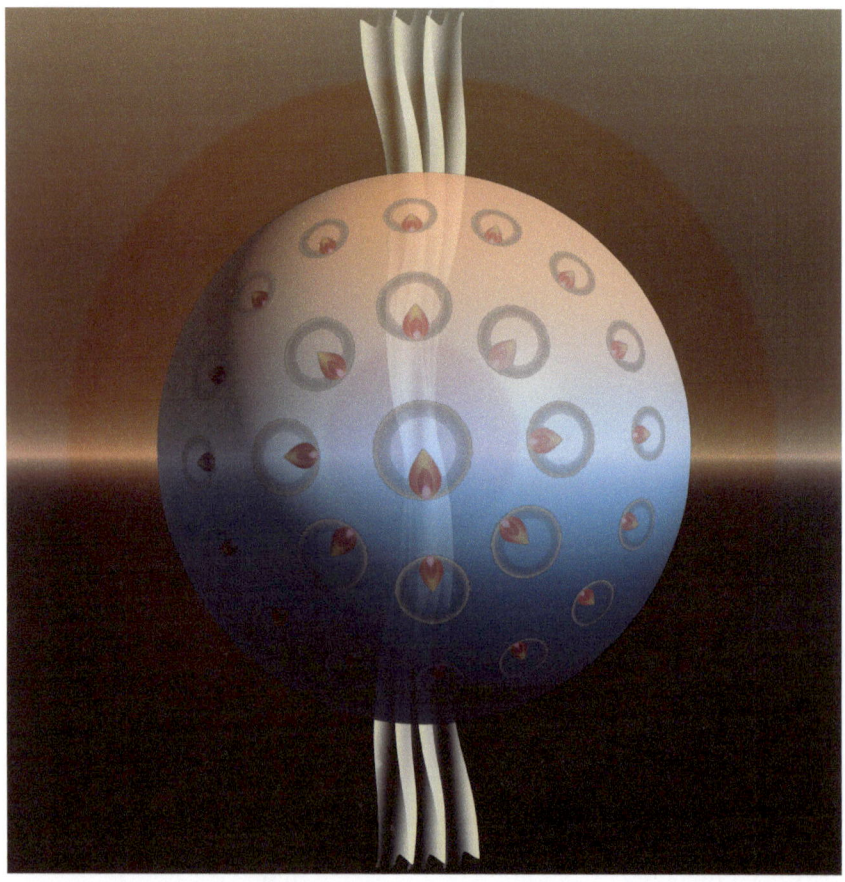

#29: Earth-Flame's Ode to Infinity

The flame around which Earth is organized was envisioned to hold a special quality. Whilst there have been many descents of light — c, c-World embryo, space-time-energy-gravity, the ever-present priest, the electromagnetic edge of light, quantum particles, atoms, cells — all necessary for the unimaginable play in c-World embryo, Earth-flame is a portal allowing continued progressive dynamics held together by a single cohesive material body.

Because of the inner creative Flame through which infinite new possibilities step forth, Earth has many names — Gaia, Tera Mater, Pachamama, Prithvi, Earth-Mother — hardly able to contain all that she is and all that she will be in the cosmic scheme.

The Glory envisioned by that **transcendent Eye**, of which all Light is only a simple outpouring between blink and blink, embodies something of itself in Earth-Flame.

That inner flame means that anything that is itself not of a fundamentally progressive nature will eventually be transformed in her fire. In the infinity of light, perhaps even in the mysterious stillness behind the transcendent Eye from which all light emanated, material aspects of **He** and **She**, destined to grow just as **Earth** herself grows, were missioned to Earth so that all in c-World embryo, would eventually partake of the full and infinite nature of Light.

The incessant burning marks the moments and establishes the rhythm in earth-time that sings forever, its Ode to Infinity.

#30: The Veritable Creators of History

Earth-Flame's Ode to Infinity is justified. For, earth is going to be the place where the great cosmic drama is determined. Perhaps this has always been the case. Perhaps in previous earth-episodes, the play of personalities led to pralayas.

But now all is different. She has come now in a way that is different. She has been called by Him. But He in his material aspect. That call means that there is the possibility of the entire cosmos participating in a material transformation. Otherwise, there would have been no need for them to come in material form.

But they have been present on earth since time immemorial. Their presence has been in forms historical and decisive — and that has to be the case.

Of the nature of Light, endowed with the destiny of Light, compelled to materialize its infinity in visible form so that all wonder that exists in infinity can express itself in creations of unending wonder, they have had to navigate possibility and push circumstance in alignment with destiny of light, so that that which can be, must be.

They have been the veritable creators of history, past, and future.

#31: The Greatest of Historical Events

The greatest of historical events, following the long play of historical events shaped by the ever-present and material Him and Her, will no doubt be the end of physical death. But that is no trivial matter.

The **flame at the center** of the earth will have to see as the eye beyond time and space sees. And then it will have to see deathless forms created around kindred flames. And it will have to open the doorway for these flames to step forth, in bodies with no strain of darkness.

But for this to happen, the kindred flames will have to have married Light incarnate. New weddings in which the children of the earth — parts and projections of He who has been on earth since time immemorial — will have to marry Victorious Her. Her, close to the fullness of She, so that She Herself can descend in them.

But that will already mean that He in his aspect of the Guiding Light, not in his aspect of the growing earth-flame, will have to have called the fullness that She is so that more of who She is can descend in Her that grows on earth.

Then the greatest of historical events — the end of physical death — will be close.

Part 4: The Dawn of Flame-Beings

#32: Flame-Being's Matter

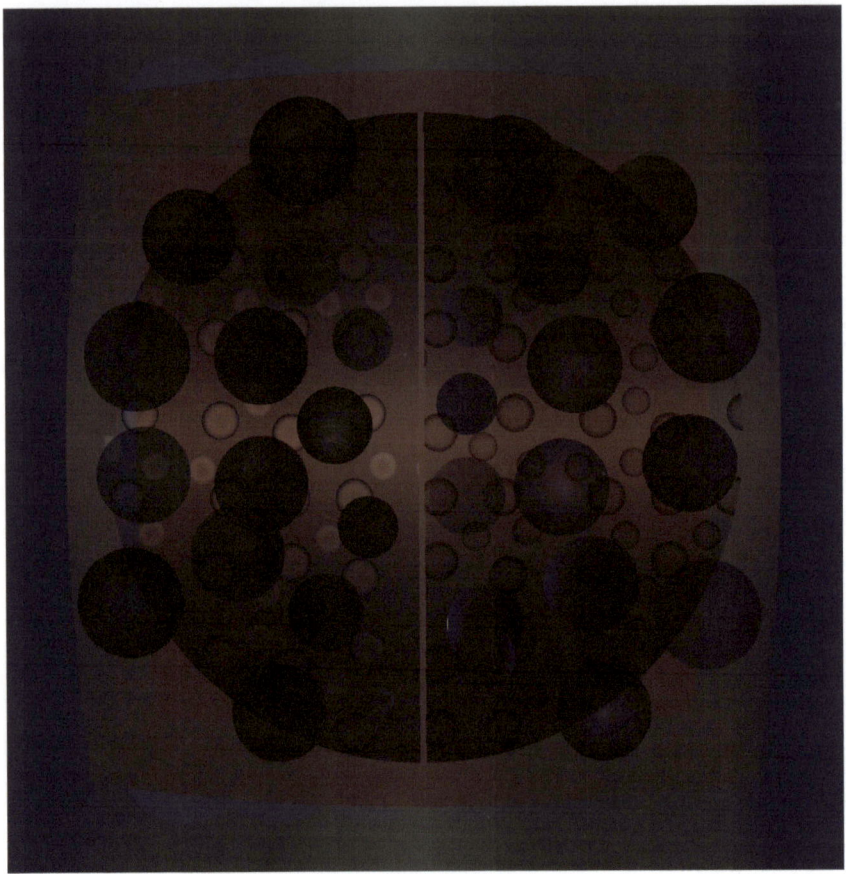

Against the pull of the **dark bosom**, the first miraculous stability was a Mind — an organized set of thoughts, perceptions, overriding principles, and way of thinking that allowed persistence of material manifestation.

The problem, though, was that that mind was veritably a *Mind of Darkness*, and gave to matter its deep fears, movements of distrust, belief in death, and its belief that it itself will not survive beyond a certain duration.

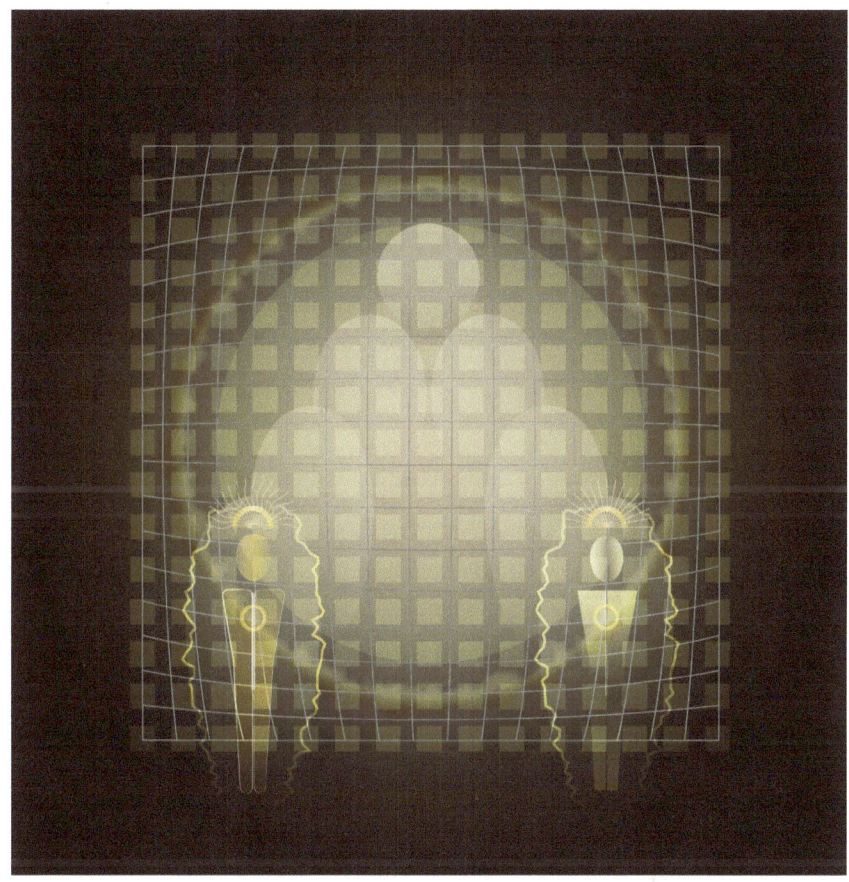

But as the **greatest of historical event** draws near, and as flame-beings incarnate, the very contract with the dark bosom comes to an end, and the very basis of matter gets organized around Light.

This in no small measure pushed by the need of the flame-beings to have a different material basis by which to operate. For matter — for the flame-beings — will need to be able to expand to the size of the Cosmos, mix with other bodies, be capable of displaying infinity…

The default way of operating, the implicit impulse in matter must change then from its being held by a mind of darkness to its being founded on Light.

#33: The New Era of Being-Possibility

Earth-beings arriving at earth-flames attract new possibilities to the material plane. Till now, there has been a plethora of functionality manifest as huge variety of rocks, plants, animals, and the individuality of human beings, only. These all show some aspects of the interplay of the endless function of the deeper, fourfold properties of Light.

The expression of function due to the **Mind of Darkness** has always been mixed and has been rather a signal flare or a brief meteorite disappearing in the immensity of night. But with the arrival of earth-flames dressed in different matter, one formed by the directness of light and in which no strain of darkness can exist, there is something extraordinarily beautiful and brilliant, a different genre of peoples, that has come into being.

This new creation shines differently, and the nature of its light becomes a beacon that calls across the cosmos and across even the antecedent layers of light governed by different macro-beings.

Allured by the call, these beings now want to come to earth, want to partake of the new adventure that is unfolding, and so is taken a bold step. Earth-flames couple with typal-lights — those prehistoric gods of antecedent layers, to begin a new era of being-possibility.

#34: Unlikely Marriages

The **New Era of Being Possibility** signals the beginning of infinitely different varieties of people. If rocks and plants and birds and animals were already numerous, if human individuality is already mind-boggling, now starts the time where flame-beings growing into cosmic possibility - to start with, - can have one foot on earth and the other on a distant Jupiter in a remote galaxy far from the Milky Way.

For it is the time where the dynamics of beings in antecedent planes couple with individualized earth-flame beings, making extraordinary dynamics exercised by individual beings bound by **earth-flame's matter** real.

Possibility now is no longer bound by death-bound matter. Instead, matter begins to get governed by possibility. And as new possibility is tried, new forms come into being.

Flame-beings expand progressively. Progressive possibility may begin by uniting with rock or plant, or bird, or animal, of flying like a shark through desert-based sand-dunes, but sooner or later inevitably join with beings from other layers of light.

These unlikely marriages remind flame-beings - materialized light-individualities - of all that the great Ascendant, native Light, is capable of, spurring them from mastery to mastery.

#35: Galactic Colonization

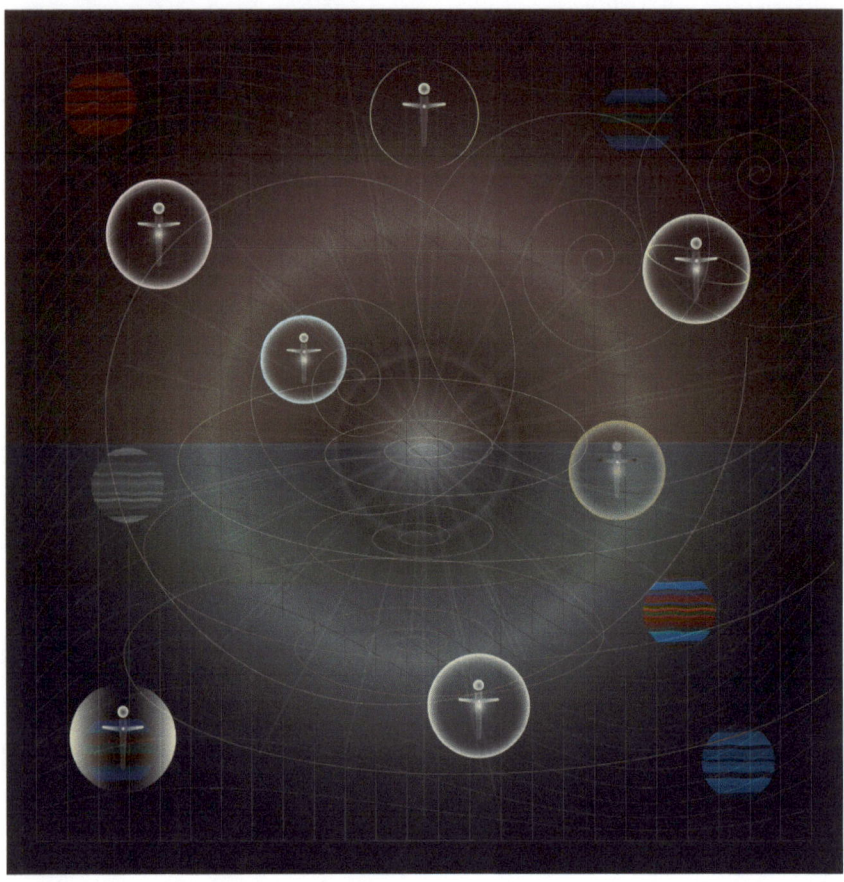

The appetite of Light to express itself is endless. Light, after all, projected from its **native state**, has somewhere within it access to the memory of what it once was.

Infinite endlessness, infinite variety, packed once into that subtle and barely even thinkable light-matrix, escapes now in potent-possibility, born of individualized **flame-beings**, initiating ever-fantastic materialization of all it held within itself.

As that possibility, living now in materialized flame-forms expands beyond earth's boundaries. The urge to unite with different star-systems, even to start new star-systems, becomes real.

In extraordinary acts of **ever-present priest** initiated, antecedent-being fulfilled, teleportation, aspiring flame-beings merge with distant nebulous haze — the cradles of to-be star-systems — extending their consciousness to start anew, individualized galactic evolution.

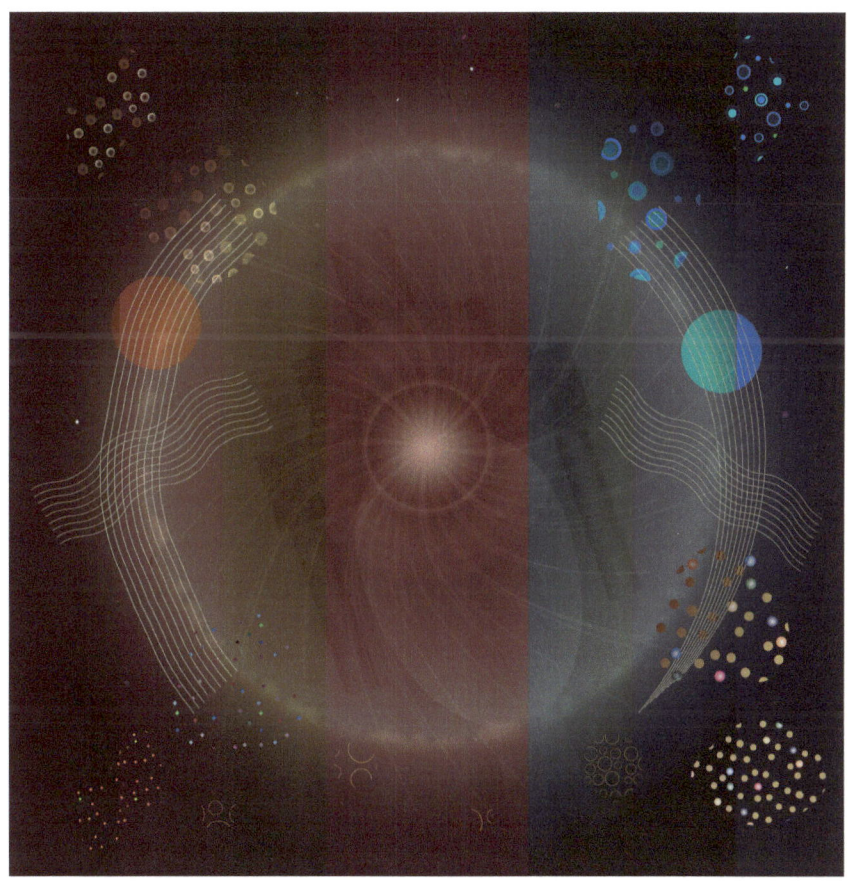

Unprecedented galactic colonization begins.

#36: Earth's Cosmic Tree of Light

The tree of life that sprouted once on earth culminated in **flame-beings**. Up until the emergence of flame-beings the plethora of light-based function was short-lived: meteorites whose flame inevitably burnt up the matter that expressed it.

But with the birth of flame-beings, a new tree of life has emerged. The seed of this tree, destined to become the Cosmic Tree of Light, is formed by light itself and cannot be stained by forms of darkness. That is its significance.

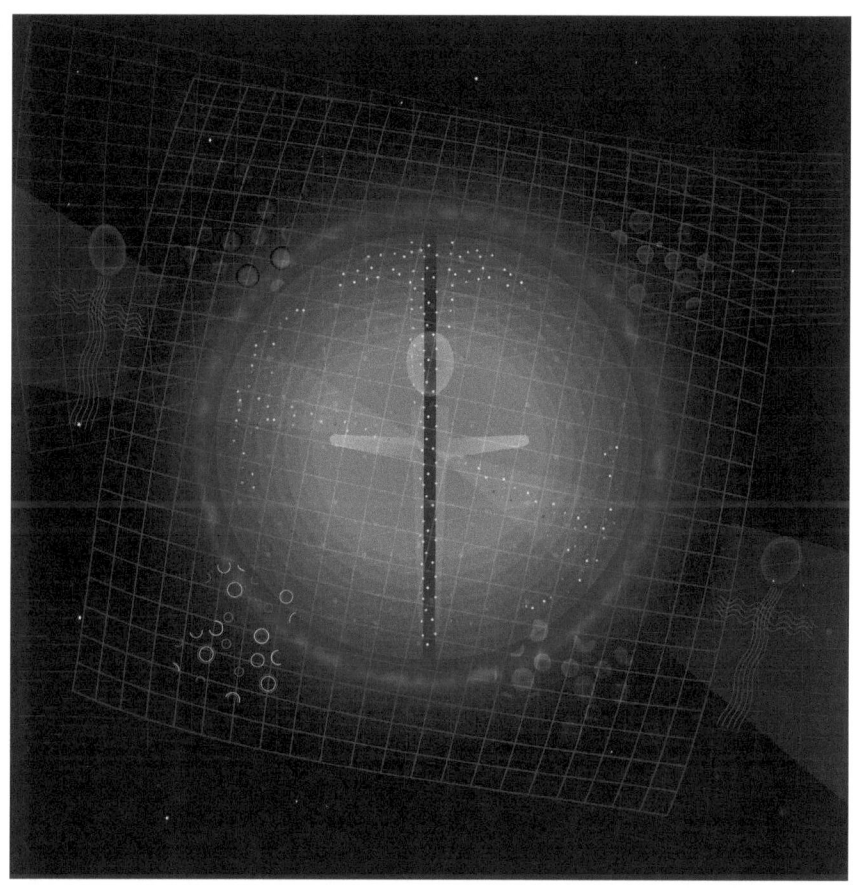

It knows not the dark things that are the stuff of earth's initial tree of life. Instead, its seed of light means that it will expand as light expands, its expansion driven by recollection of all the possibility that lives forever in the light-matrix at infinity.

And as it expands, it bares variety of different fruit that themselves start cycles of never-before-seen star-clusters and star-beings: beings of light, who grow forever into more forms of light, by the infinite power of light itself.

#37: The Once Existing Tree of Life

Once upon a time, Light needed a material laboratory in which to grow its first possibilities. **Earth** was that chosen place. Light started small, and earth's tree of life emerged. Already this tree of life was extraordinary. For whereas in different star-systems spread far and wide across the cosmos, life existed, it existed as typal-life bound forever to what it was.

This typal stability, through cosmic entanglement, allowed evolutionary form on earth to connect in some sub-space to the type it represented. And on earth, by the force of light, one form eventually transitioned into another until earth-born form could merge with something more significant of **Her** and become **flame-being**.

And with the emergence of flame-being, **Earth's Cosmic Tree of Light** was born. Being coupled with different types of even antecedent-layer being and cased in new light-based matter, this matter remained fresh and flexible to the will and possibility held by flame-beings.

All manner of flame-being based living-form emerged. And as the flame-being forms stepped through solar systems, eventually, new star-systems coupled with their extraordinary consciousness came into being.

Death here existed not. It couldn't since even new, and early forms in these individualized galactic evolutions knew not of it. For these, it was just a remote phenomenon sung about sometimes in association with memories of the once existing tree of life.

#38: Once-Typal Worlds

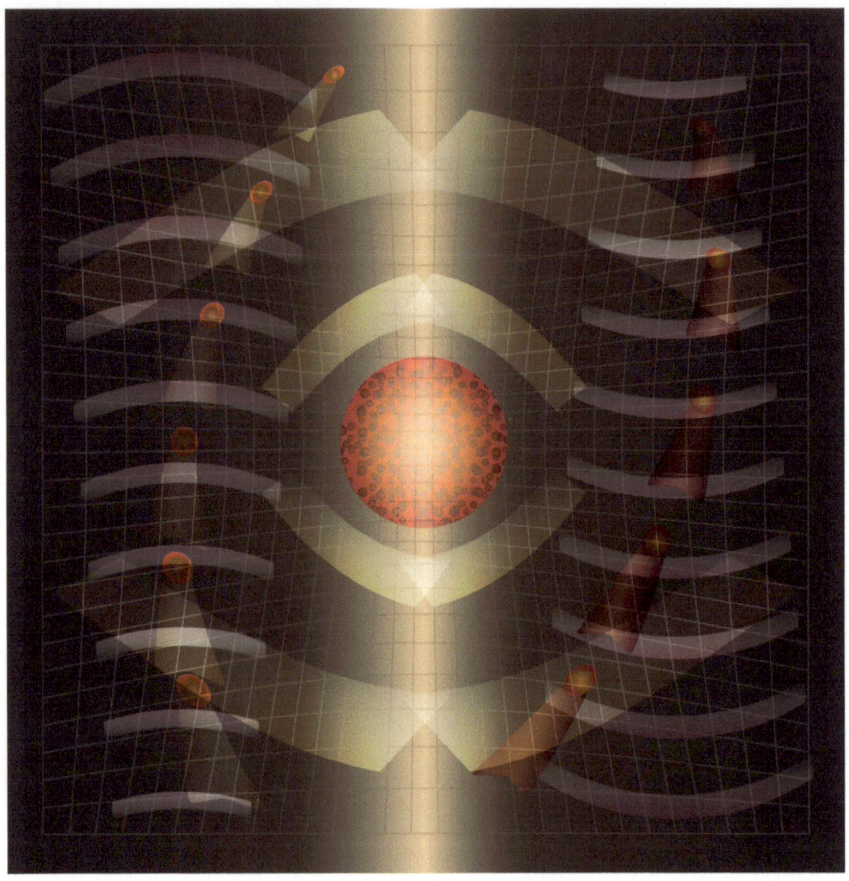

With evolutionary possibility seeded in **new star-clusters** by flame-beings from the growing **Cosmic Tree of Light**, the earth-confined experiment of evolution could now be spread across Cosmos.

Now with the successful spread of individualized lines of galactic consciousness, star clusters and their planetary systems housed unforeseen and unimagined flame-beings who **knew not death**. Life unfolded in spectacular and unique displays of light-possibility.

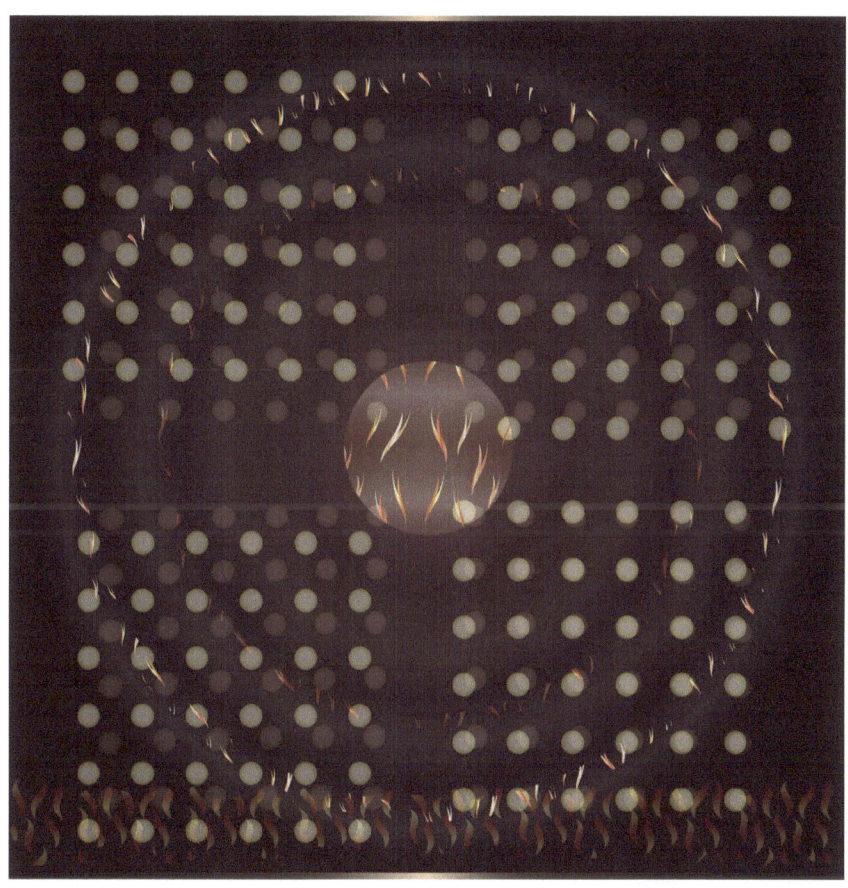

Entanglement due to spreading lines of galactic consciousness crossed the threshold value, releasing tides of evolutionary possibility that rippled through the vast population of typal star-systems and planets. Beings there felt the flaming forth of unknown aspirations from the even young fires lit somewhere within.

The very foundations of Cosmos opened to Earth's Cosmic Tree of Light, and strange new seeds destined to sprout, perhaps in a plethora of **undreamed marriages**, were sown in now once-typal worlds.

#39: The Veritable Material Holiday

The call that calls forth something more of Infinity, that call that compels secrets of Light to manifest by leaps and bounds, that call that causes Her to reveal more of who She is, sounded again as typal existence was overcome by evolutionary reality, which rippled throughout the Cosmos.

The Tree of Light had emerged and continued to spread its branches. Its fruit was getting seeded everywhere. As galaxies and star-clusters began evolutionary journeys from light to greater light, and as typal systems awoke to an aspiring flame, the very foundation of the Cosmos changed.

Even if the greatest of antecedent beings had wanted to remain aloof or looked with discontent at the material universe because of its paucity, that now was changed. They could step into matter, which, having been formed from greater and greater content of Light, would morph more easily to their inner need.

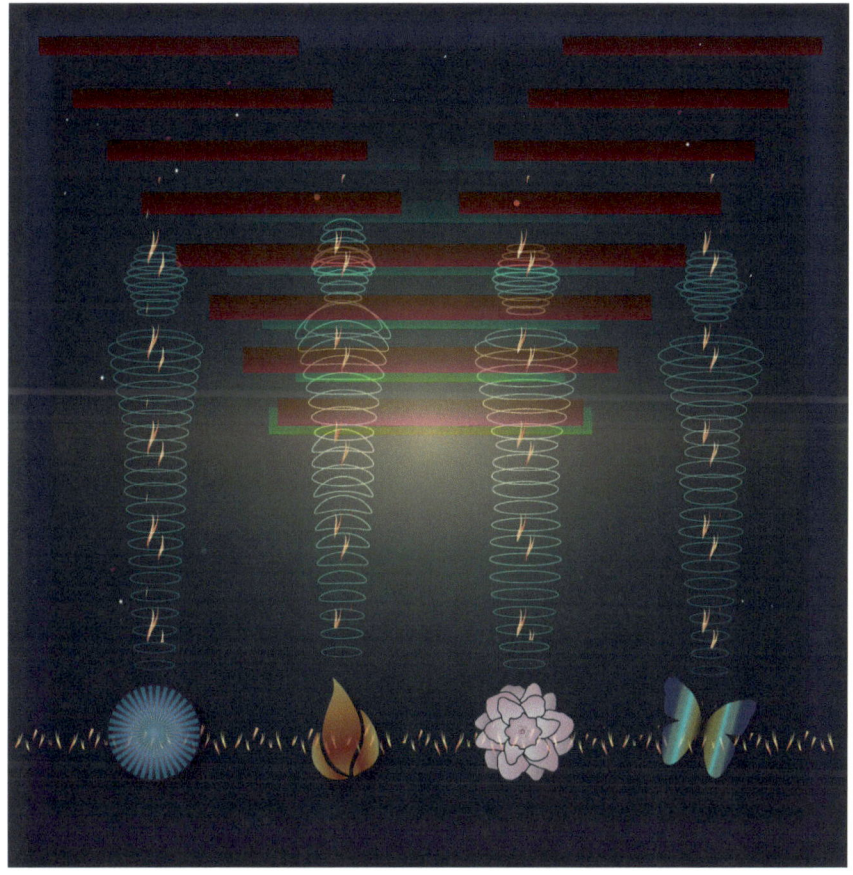

They could descend into the material universe and perhaps even enjoy the manifestation without getting bogged down by it. Rocks could be made to chirp and fly on wings of courage, and a pink-rose smile could be made to grow from within them by the urge expressed at the tetrahedral crystal level.

Even the greatest of antecedent beings would experience a veritable material holiday in the emerging new Cosmos.

Part 5: The New Cosmos

#40: Space-Time-Energy-Gravity Mounds

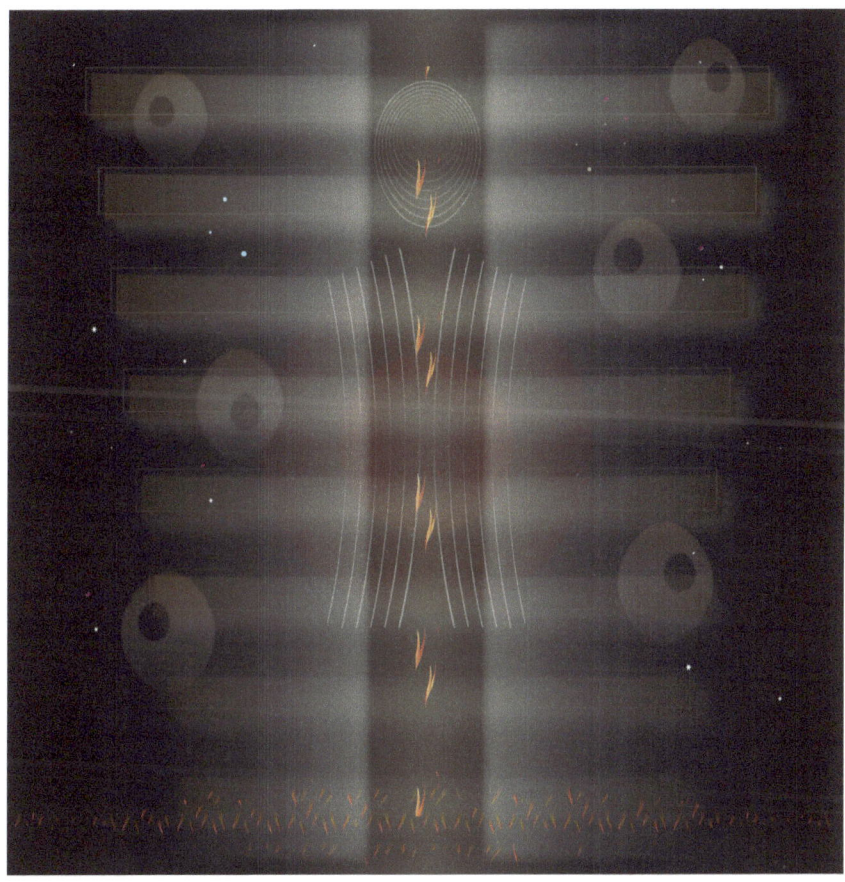

The **ever-present priest**, omnipresent within the **space-time-energy-gravity container**, just used to take certain light-filled inner urges to the antecedent realms as offering to those powerful beings resident there. In this way, something more of their substance would be compelled to inform the subtle material fields and sooner or later change material manifestation based on the initiating light-filled urges.

But now dynamics had altered, and instead of the vertical journey, there was a newer horizontal journey that the ever-present priest would engage in. With the **Cosmic Tree of Light** spreading its branches, fruit, and the birth of new possibilities aligned with light across the cosmos, the power to deeply change material things did not anymore just reside in antecedent layers of light.

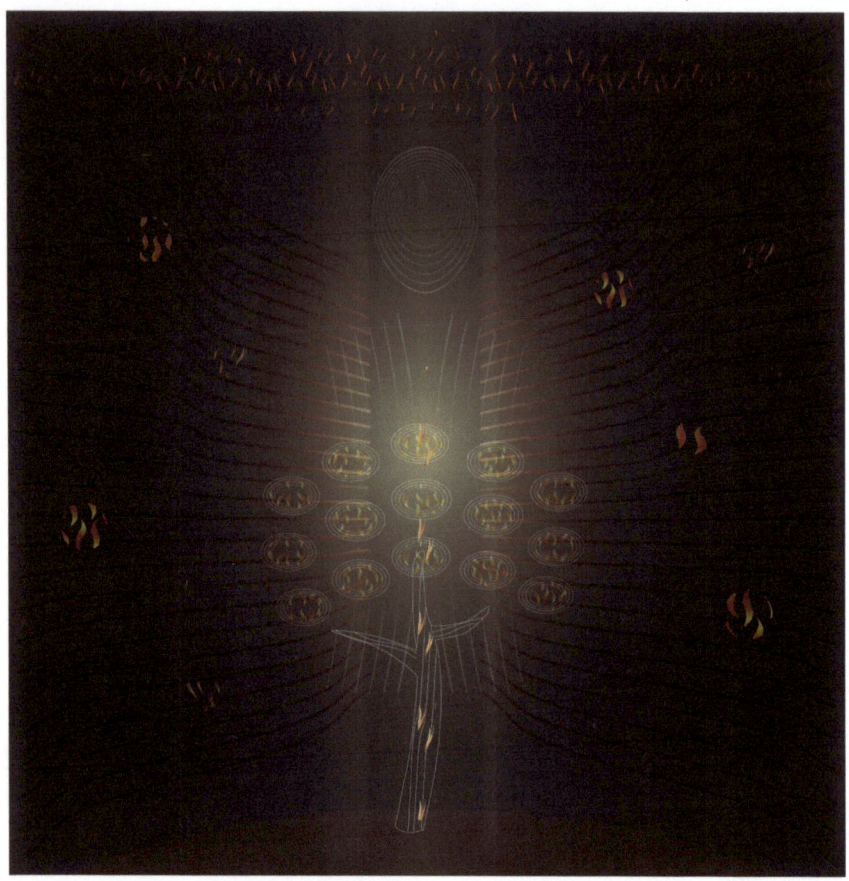

Now that ability had been birthed into the physical cosmos, and the ever-present priest, through the magic of his power, built channels emanating from new galactic possibility to numerous space-time-energy-gravity mounds. These space-time-energy-gravity mounds held within themselves the dynamics of material change from the initiating galactic centers, allowing that same change to take place multiply, in defiance of all old laws of the velocity of change.

The nature of space-time-energy-gravity was changing. New law could be written faster, empowered by the greater presence of light across the cosmos and the container.

#41: Amorem Particles

Fundamental changes in the foundations of the cosmos accelerated through the spread of the Cosmic Tree of Light, the space-time-energy-gravity mounds, and veritable antecedent being material holidays, allow different cosmic conditions to come into being.

That mysterious initial plunge of light into darkness held in itself wonders implicit in its native state. The force of love bound all emergences so that implicit reality folded in light, sought even explicitly to maintain something of what it was. Love was that binding factor that allowed knowledge-based quarks, power-based leptons, harmony-based bosons, and the presence-based Higgs-boson to bind together even explicitly to create a foundational wonder.

But now, because of the foundational changes, Love itself came out from behind the veil in a new category of *love-based amorem particles*. This gives new power to multiversity. For it is now not just four powers of light arranging themselves in endless copies of themselves, but a fifth that is a master-key.

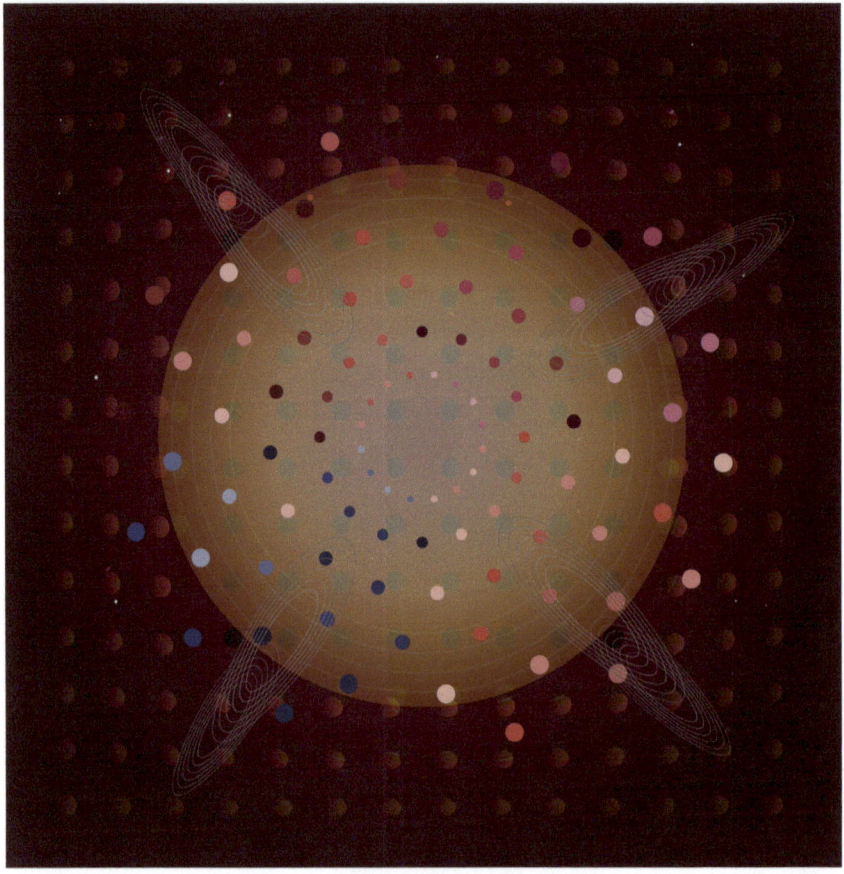

Its surfacing allows what is deep within to express itself materially without. Quantum multiverses can combine in unexpected ways allowing untold possibilities to surface materially.

#42: 108,000 Function-Foldedness Atomic-Equilibria

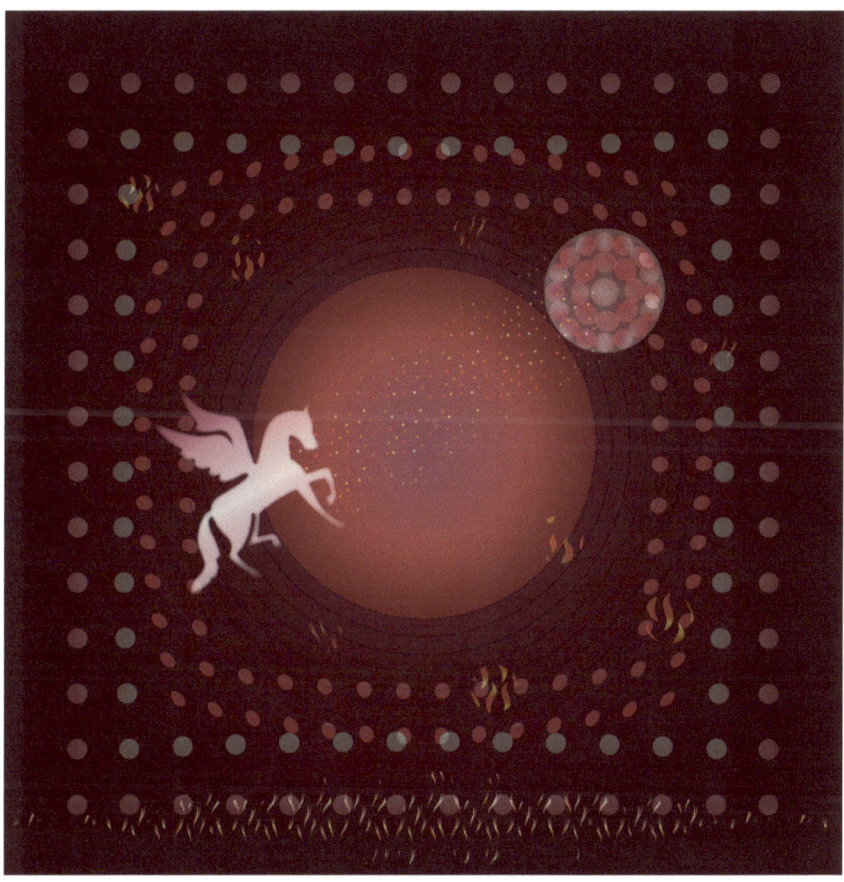

Quantum multiverses imbued with the explicit power of love allow all manner of combinations to come into being. Pink-winged horses that in mid-flight spread themselves in waves of joy across the cosmos before landing on a distant asteroid, thus changing it to diamond, is an unlikely outcome made real due to the nature of distinct multiverses coming together to materially express unknown possibilities.

The precious 108-bead atom necklace, held by matter as it chanted its cosmic call inviting combination of functions to express itself as molecules and myriad forms of life, can in an instant change into a 108,000-bead wonder, dazzling creation with the vast diversity of astounding atom-based equilibria. Extraordinary function, not just antecedent-based but also sourced from possibility being birthed from **individualized galactic adventures in consciousness**, create atoms of unfathomed complexity as five-fold quantum particles coalesce in unforeseen combinations.

And as with the amorem particles, 108,000 function-foldedness is only possible with the surfacing of the fifth type of atom, beyond the power-based s-Group atoms, beyond the knowledge-based p-Group atoms, beyond the presence-based d-Group atoms, and beyond the harmony-based f-Group atoms, in the body of the *love-based a-Group atoms*.

The love-based a-Group atoms invite vast love-based function into the layers of atomic-equilibria and defy all chemical experience allowing impossible combinations of existing atoms to take place.

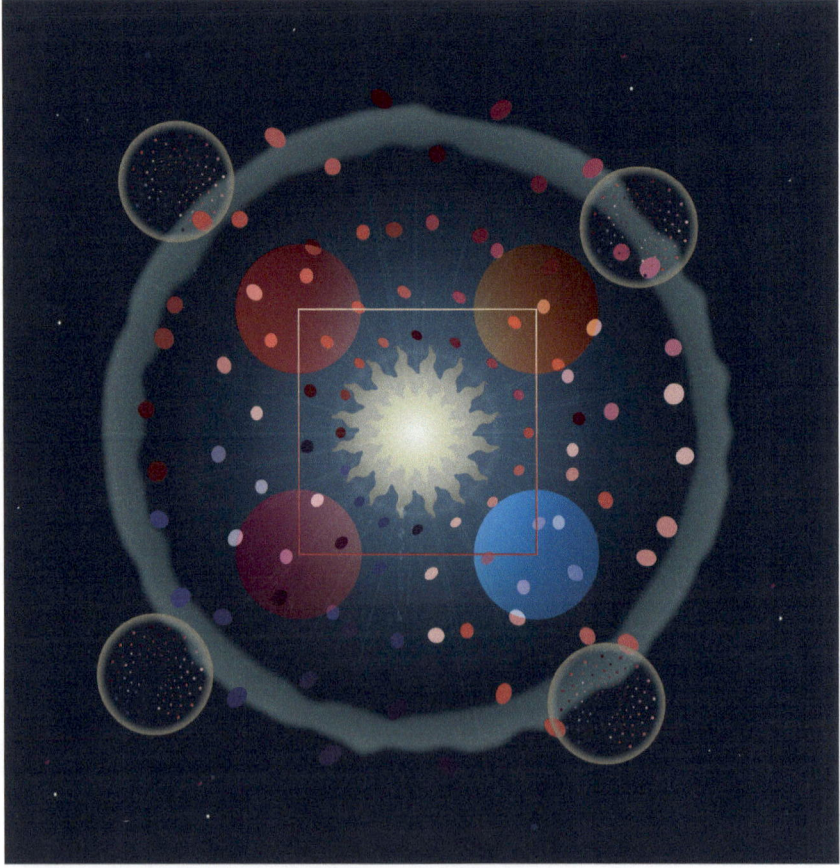

Thus it is that 108,000 function-foldedness can come into being.

#43: Love-Found Cells

Five-foldness expressing itself in quantum particles and in atoms is the bases for cell-based five-foldness to come into being. This five-foldness, seen in the Eye from which all comes, was long-awaited and required many conditions to be met: many descents, many sacrifices, many victories, many marriages…

But now the miracles are done and this new miracle, signaling a new era of Light, where the cell itself gains union with all that is in Cosmos, with all that is Cosmos, with that even that is hidden by Cosmos, becomes real.

For the fifth molecular plan, that beyond knowledge-based nucleic acids, that beyond presence-based proteins, that beyond power-based polysaccharides, that beyond harmony-based lipids, riding on the back of amorem-particles, riding on the back of a-Group atoms and the myriad molecules created from 108,000 function-foldedness, manifests now in the vehicle of *love-based Anandam*.

And this love-based anandam allows cells to veritably love all creation. Cells can now expand unendingly without losing their selves, cells can merge with all other material manifestations, cells can pass through all other material manifestations as a flirtatious breeze passes through the now swaying branches of a blushing tree, cells can morph into an infinity of shapes, cells can express feeling through a range of color, cells become instruments for Love itself…

#44: Fractal Fullness

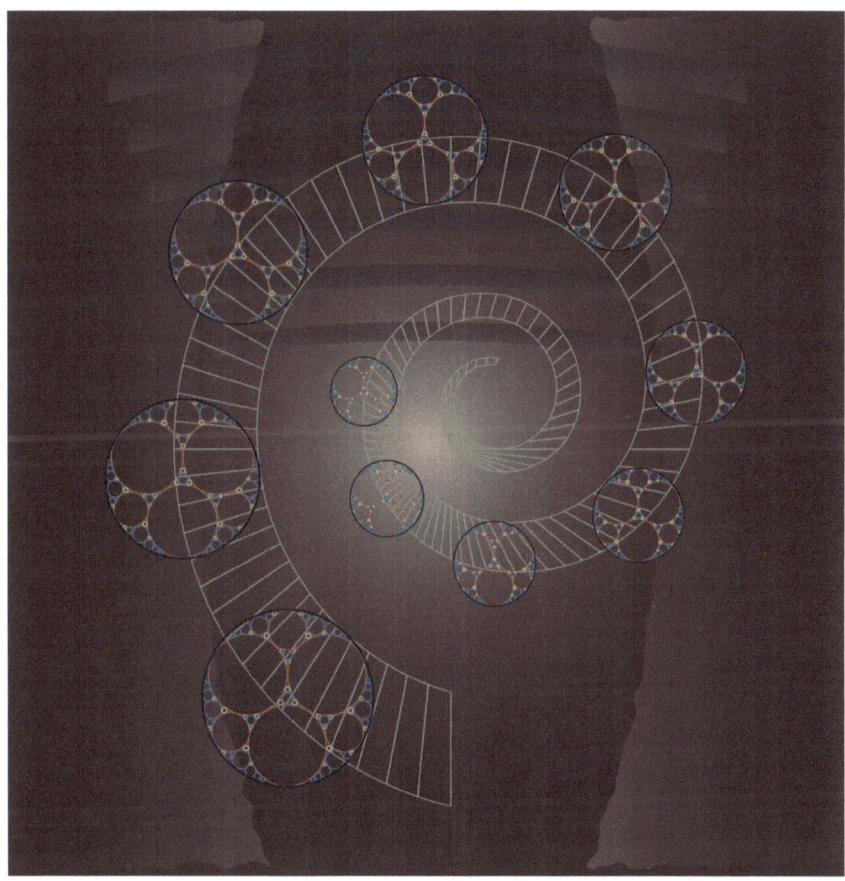

What is Infinity? A true glimpse can be provided by material manifestation that begins to yield to its possibilities. That, after all, is what the Cosmos is — an adventure in yielding to all the possibility **resident in Light**. And with the five-foldness manifest now in **quantum-particle**, **atom**, and **cell**, something of what it is can be more fully experienced materially.

For life, based on five-fold cells can morph and fly, disappear and reappear in new forms while all the time holding Love and Light and all the gifts that come with it. It can expand to the limits of Cosmos, interact with antecedent layers of light, and make incarnate in matter all manner of wonder.

But the keystroke of manifestation is not just union with all that is, but also a precise display of unique individualities in an infinity of diversity that yet is one with the Oneness that is.

Materially that would mean that each manifested individual would be able to — because of the extraordinary flexibility, plasticity, and adaptability of the five-fold molecular plan-based cells — reflect materially any and all other individuality in whatever manifested form, such that that individual's material expression remained centered around that unique individual, that unique flame-being that that individual is.

Trees and planets, distant galaxies even, in addition to whatever combination of individual flame-beings, would now materially become some expression of what these are in the material body of the unique flame-being, exercising the right to be in a new balance of all or some aspects of all with one, anchored deeply still in the One Light of which all are varied expressions.

Fractal fullness became a new property of material manifestation.

#45: The Surrender of Quanta and the Being of Speed

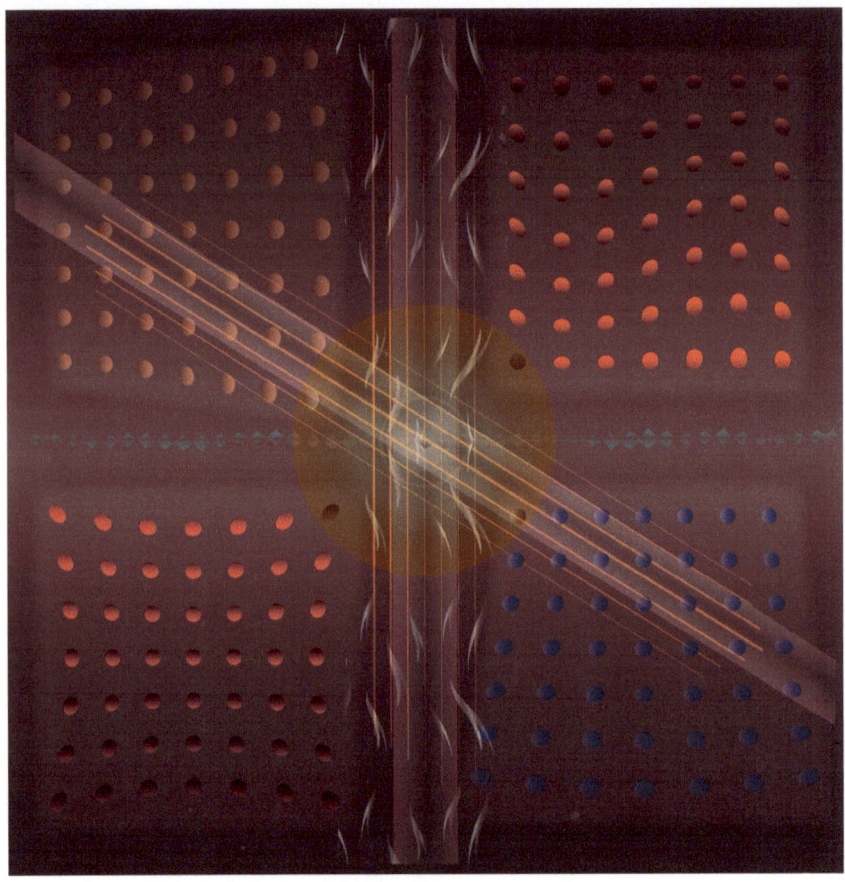

In the mystery of material manifestation, Quanta has played a key role in bringing out what is in Possibility. The Being of Speed lent himself to the devices of Light, providing the physical means by which quanta and her contents could come into being.

For as light first sought to make more objective its **massive implicit content** that was all as One where it traveled infinitely fast, it merged with the Being of Speed who made light slowdown in some projected reality that gave way now to a new set of dynamics. As light slowed down, more of what was in it became visible through quanta. Each quantum, requiring a finite speed of light to express itself, disclosed the mystery that it held within its bosom.

And as the Being of Speed continued to apply his magic to project Light at a slower speed, quanta became pregnant in yet another way, giving birth to more of what was in Light, until light slowed down to the miraculous speed of c, that speed that allowed the cosmic adventure to unfold in the way that it has.

And now that material manifestation is more fully alive with Her possibilities, now that the Cosmic Tree of Light has spread, now that individualized galactic consciousness can express itself in unique lines of evolution, now that antecedent beings of Light can experience veritable material holidays, now that space-time-energy-gravity mounds abound across Cosmos, now that five-foldness is alive with the birth of amorem particles, l-Group atoms, and anandam molecular plans, now that cells can equal cosmos, the need for the Being of Speed to uphold the schema of layered light, the need for Quanta to give birth through time-bound pregnancy, has been transcended.

In a reversal of cosmic habit, the Being of Speed and Quanta surrendered themselves and merged into material manifestation, gifting it with their powers and with a master stroke setting the scene for an even greater display of the Possibilities of Light.

#46: Matter's Role in Empress-Emperor-Hood

With the surrender of Quanta and the Being of Speed, great gifts are embedded into material possibility. Manifestation following the vision of the Eye does not need to be striated anymore. All layers of light merge and exist as one.

The gifts implicit in light at infinite speed, the gifts implicit in light projected at various finite speeds, the very dynamics of all that these different layers of light expressed, can now merge in the layer of light that exists at speed c. Antecedent and c-Layer Beings hence enter into a new cosmic community. Brothers and sisters clasp in an embrace that seals the meaning of matter.

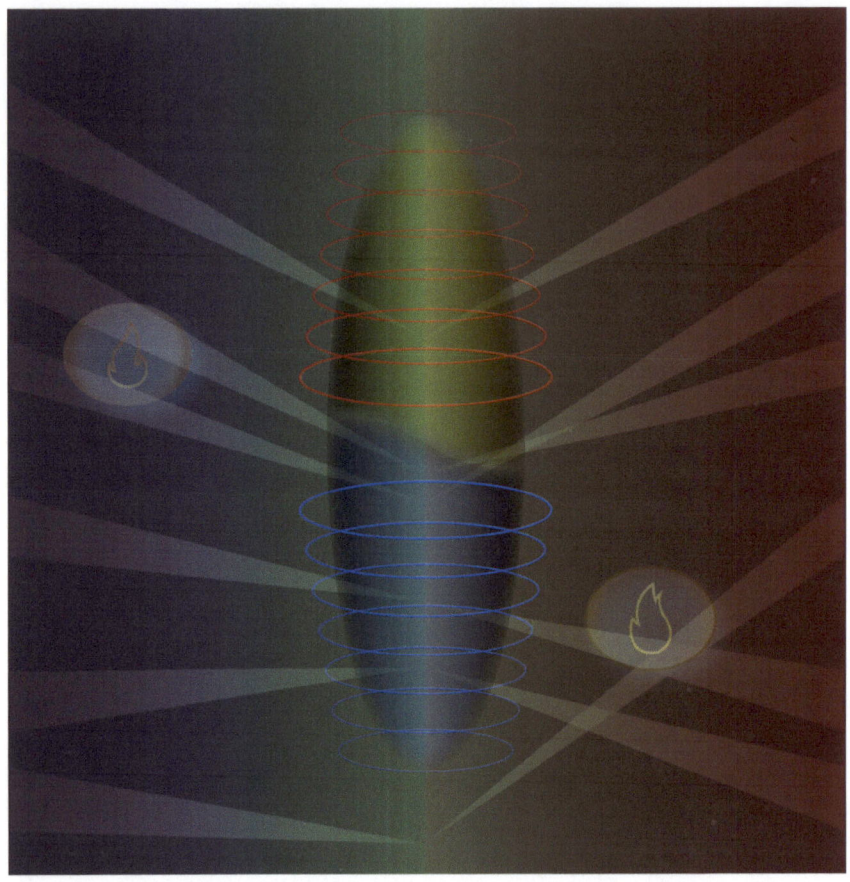

Once meta-thought and once distant idea occurring here in c-Layer, and once c-Layer thought and c-Layer idea now each has the same power to shape matter. Matter becomes a means by which any aspect of Light can be expressed materially.

Spirit, that which was thought of as the subtle processes of Light in its native state where it traveled infinitely fast, displaying omnipresence, omnipotence, omniscience, and omninurturance, is now defined by Matter. Matter and that which was Spirit are One and create the means by which royal Empress-Emperor-hood will express full dominion over all of Light's vicinities.

#47: He & She

With matter's new reality, the age-old romance between He and She reaches new heights. He had come to earth as the potent forerunner of **flame-beings** eons ago. His growth was tied to **Earth-Flame's** growth. He was none other than Earth's soul. She had come too as His flame-being's counterpart calling down more of Her who watched all from above.

He and She are there as one above, and their coming to Earth was so that Earth could become the resplendent material Queen-King-Dom of Light. Through the making of history and the greatest of historical events, resulting in the birth of flame-beings, matter itself went through a decisive change, one in which death did not have to be.

Now all manner of **light-beings married with flame-beings** preparing an even greater marriage between flame-beings and Her. In this way, a new Cosmic Tree of Light emerged and spread across the cosmos, changing the destiny of even distant galaxies.

Matter's role in Empress-Emperor-Hood, following five-foldness manifest in amorem particles, l-Group atoms, anandam molecular plans, and cells equivalence to Cosmos, allowed all to yield to Their command. The throne was installed, and He and She could reign now as double-ruler over all material realms of Light.

#48: Infinitesimal Material Universes

With **Their double-reign**, all commands would be fulfilled. Nothing that They had ever dreamed of would remain unfulfilled. Such was their power. And their power meant that even infinitesimal spaces bound by infinitesimal time would have all infinity enfolded in it as material reality.

The Child watching the drop of water that seems to journey forever would be able to see worlds in those drops. And in those worlds, the Child watching the drops would be able to see worlds in those even more space-bound, time-bound drops.

And this would continue ad infinitum. And the Child being the offspring of Her-Him that now was the double-ruler over all material realm, would be curious to spiral the cycle in new ways — that cycle that started with an initial opening of **an Eye**. But what is that Eye, and in what bounds does matter now exist? For every cycle can be seen as none other than to assure full material wonder forever and ever into the depths that at any time can open to all of Light.

The Child plays and becomes the double-ruler. And in that play, new material possibilities arise.

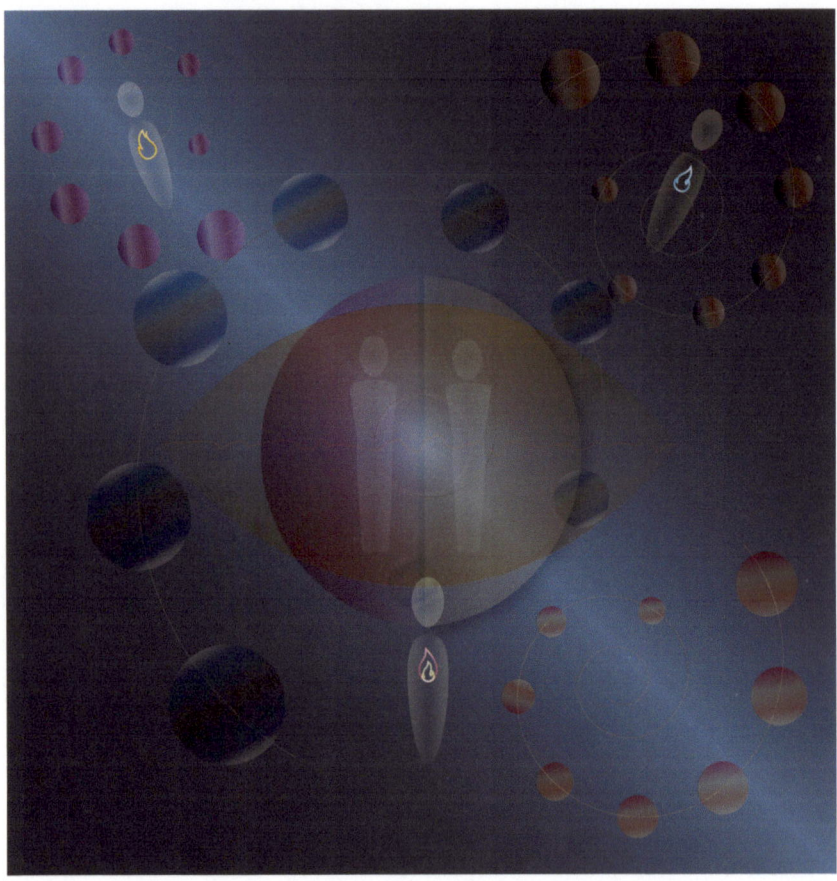

#49: Inexpressible Domains of Light

There was a time when the gravitation of darkness due to overt and hidden **Titan rule** would overpower any attempt at moving toward Light. The great dark Dragon would lash its tail, and all **love-enabled matter** would reel back into the **dark bosom**. Then the journey from **pralaya** would need to begin again.

But by descent upon descent and miracle upon miracle, more of **Her** reign became materially real, assuring the **end of the path to pralaya**. Even then, earlier in the manifestation, She brought about the end of death and the **flowering of all Cosmos** in unique paths to Light.

Matter itself was One and the Only. All dreams and manner of dreams and all high command would find it the perfect means to express splendor. Matter was nothing other than an extension of Light. **Matter was Light.** And all continued to advance by leaps and bounds following **Their double-reign.** Even **infinitesimal adventure** reflected unending mystery and possibility whilst always on the safe foundation of Light.

The Holiday of Light, teeming with fullness, was a pipeline to all that remained Unknowable in the realm behind that **Eye's flash of Light.** And in periods of mysterious out-flashes, something of the Unknown precipitated into the material visible domains of Light, assured by its extraordinarily developed receptivity, to project it unexpectedly further into inexpressible domains of Light.

#50: The March of Matter's Mystery

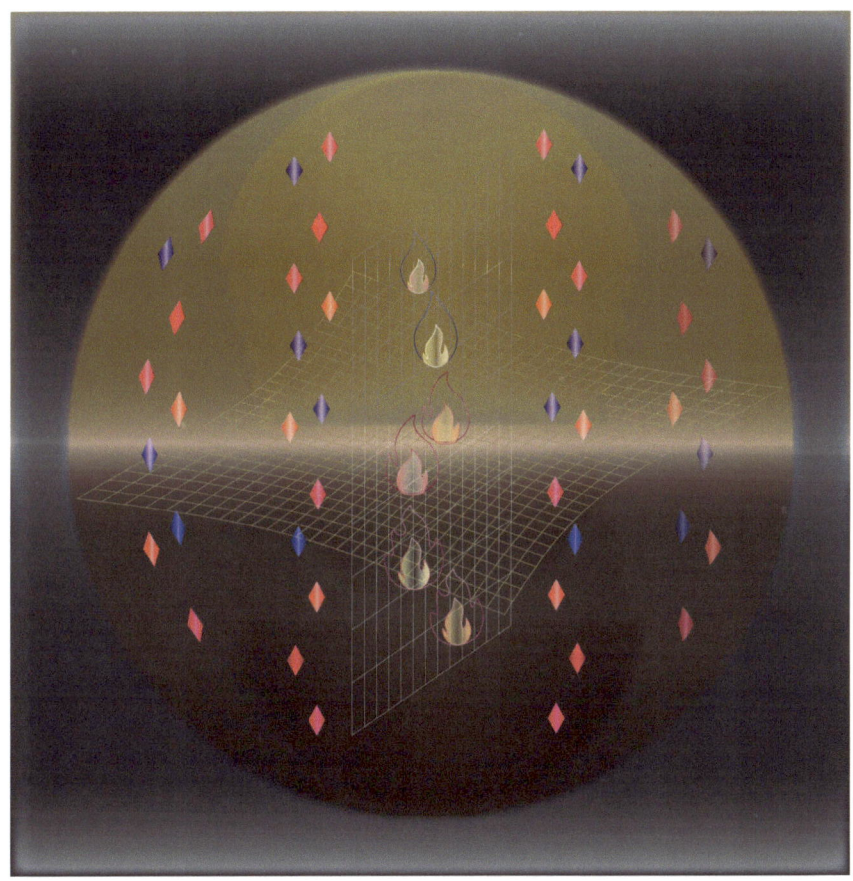

The advance in Light, assured by **Their Double-Reign**, bought the cosmos closer to the Unknowable. The Unknowable now had entries into the Knowable and could alter its trajectory without any loss of purpose because so much of light had come forward to continue to change the very foundations of Cosmos.

Gods could arise in all material splendor at a moment's notice, and all of Cosmos would be ready to express and reflect the new impulses introduced by that movement. Matter itself was Spirit, and all of Light existed in the least of its material fronts.

There was infinite depth to Matter, and all of Light could find a resting place and vast dynamic playing-fields regardless of how infinitesimal bounds became. Individuality was an extraordinary flower whose petals could reveal all Cosmos, and Cosmos could show infinite faces of itself in a moment.

The Unknowable and the Knowable, all that was Above and all Below, were now more easily interchangeable, and Matter marched splendidly forward, forever expressing infinite mystery.

Relevant Background and Follow-up Information

The Author's Early Books

1. The Flowering of Management
2. India's Contribution to Management

The Fractal Series

1. Connecting Inner Power with Global Change: The Fractal Ladder
2. Redesigning the Stock Market: A Fractal Approach
3. The Flower Chronicles: A Radical Approach to Systems and Organizational Development
4. The Fractal Organization: Creating Enterprises of Tomorrow

The Cosmology of Light Series

1. A Story of Light: A Simple Exploration of the Creation and Dynamics of this Universe and Others
2. Oceans of Innovation: The Mathematical Heart of Complex Systems
3. Emergence: A Mathematical Journey from the Big Bang to Sustainable Global Civilization
4. Quantum Certainty: A Mathematics of Natural and Sustainable Human History
5. Super-Matter: Functional Richness in an Expanding Universe
6. Cosmology of Light: A Mathematical Integration of Matter, Life, History & Civilization, Universe, and Self

The Application of Cosmology of Light Series

1. The Emperor's Quantum Computer: An Alternative Light-Centered Interpretation of Quanta, Superposition, Entanglement and the Computing that Arises from it
2. The Origins and Possibilities of Genetics: A Mathematical Exploration in a Cosmology of Light
3. The Second Singularity: A Mathematical Exploration of AI-Based and Other Singularities in a Cosmology of Light

4. Triumph of Love: A Mathematical Exploration of Being, Becoming, Life, and Transhumanism in a Cosmology of Light

The Artistic Interpretation of Cosmology of Light Series

1. The Mandala Illustrated Story of Light
2. Musings on Light: A Meditative, Non-Mathematical Summary of a Cosmology of Light
3. The Illustrated Oceans of Innovation: The Mathematical Heart of Complex Systems Depicted in Indian Arts
4. Emergence Illustrated: A Mathematical Journey from the Big Bang to Sustainable Global Civilization Depicted with Indian Mythological Arts
5. The Dawn of Flame-Beings: Mythological Musings Based on a Cosmology of Light

Note on Genesis of Books

In the earlier stage I wrote 'The Flowering of Management' and 'India's Contribution to Management'. The impetus for both these books was similar in that they were reactions to the environment that I was placed in at the time. When I first began working in the corporate world the reality of the environment struck me as decidedly anachronistic. I had a different sense of what life could offer and wrote 'The Flowering of Management' to capture aspects of a vision I thought corporations and money existed for. Similarly, when I wrote 'India's Contribution to Management' it was the result of the dissatisfaction I experienced when confronted with the prevalent interpretation of India. This was precipitated by my working with a US-based company, A.T. Kearney, in India. I sought to reverse that interpretation with 'India's Contribution to Management' which aimed to capture my understanding of the essence and deeper capacity of synthesis of India.

The next phase was marked by a strong interest in fractals that primarily stemmed from my beginning to see similar patterns in seemingly distinct areas of life. I wrote 'Connecting Inner Power with Global Change: The Fractal Ladder' as a theoretical framework of fractals. The fractals that I envisioned included the added complexities of emotional and thought components. This was followed by 'Redesigning the Stock Market: A Fractal Approach' which was an application of the theoretical fractal framework to the then recent global financial crises of 2008. 'The Flower Chronicles' sought to make the gist of the ubiquitous fractal I had described in the previous two books easily graspable at the visceral level primarily through many practical examples spanning diverse walks of life. 'The Fractal Organization: Creating Enterprises of Tomorrow' was a comprehensive summary of the fractal framework that included the basic theory, the applications, and a practical field guide that had been developed while I was working at the Organizational Development group at Stanford University Medical Center.

The most recent phase has focused on creating a mathematical framework to take the previously developed fractal framework further. The development of such a mathematical framework that seeks to frame innovation in complex adaptive systems was also the focus of my doctoral work. This gave birth to an exciting period and will result in multiple series of books.

The first series, comprising of six books, extended my inquiry into mathematics and complex adaptive systems to an interesting limit culminating in the nature of Light and the Cosmos. The fractal mathematics I propose is at the heart of this series: Cosmology of Light.

The first book, 'A Story of Light: A Simple Exploration of the Creation and Dynamics of this Universe and Others' contains the main ideas in the mathematics, in non-mathematical terms, that are further explored mathematically in the remaining books in this series. The second book 'Oceans of Innovation: The Mathematical Heart of Complex Systems' describes my interpretation of the mathematical foundation of complex systems. The third book, 'Emergence: A Mathematical Journey from the Big Bang to Sustainable Global Civilization' applies the mathematics to several layers of matter and life. The fourth book, 'Quantum Certainty: A Mathematics of Natural and Sustainable Human History' describes a process culminating in space, time, energy, and gravity quantization by which history is made. The fifth book, 'Super-Matter: Functional Richness in an Expanding Universe' describes a process for the creation of super-matter-based on a need for continued functional-richness. A link is made between the resulting quantization of space and an expanding universe. The final book, 'Cosmology of Light: A Mathematical Integration of Matter, Life, History & Civilization, Universe, and Self' proposes an integrated mathematical framework that flows through all things, hence unifying matter, light, civilization, history, universe, and self.

The second series further explores the implications of "one mathematics flowing through all things". The first book in this series 'The Emperor's Quantum Computer: An Alternative Light-Centered Interpretation of Quanta, Superposition, Entanglement and the Computing that Arises from it' describes an alternative narrative for quantum computing to the one commonly expressed today. The second book in the series, 'The Origin and Possibilities of Genetics: A Mathematical Exploration in a Cosmology of Light' explores pre-genetic, genetic, and post-genetic possibilities in a cosmology of light. This book, 'The Second Singularity: A Mathematical Exploration of AI-Based and Other Singularities in a Cosmology of Light' explores the limits of AI-based singularities with respect to light-based singularities. This book, the final in this series explores transhumanism in a cosmology of light.

The third series, Artistic Interpretation of Cosmology of Light, is intended to make Cosmology of Light more accessible by interpreting it artistically. The first book in the series is 'The Mandala Illustrated Story of Light'. The objective is to lead the reader through the story of light using mandalas as an aid in the journey. The second book 'Musings on Light' is a meditative book set to graphical illustrations. The illustrations focus on 50 key concepts derived from the ten-book joint Cosmology of Light series. The third book 'The Illustrated Oceans of Innovation: The Mathematical Heart of Complex Systems Depicted in Indian Arts' uses Indian Arts to illustrate the mathematical heart of complex systems. The fourth book 'Emergence Illustrated: A Mathematical Journey from the Big Bang to Sustainable Global Civilization Depicted with Indian Mythological Arts' uses Indian mythological arts to express the concepts of Emergence. The fifth and current is book 'The Dawn of Flame-Beings: Mythological Musings Based on a Cosmology of Light'. Several additional books are envisioned and are currently under development.

About the Author

Dr. Pravir Malik has been developing a unified theory and mathematics of organization over the last three decades. He has written 16 books related to this to emphasize a whole systems approach integrating individual, organizational, economic, social, environmental, and evolutionary dimensions. In recent years he has been intimately involved with computer modeling of complex organizational, economic, and world systems to help different stakeholders practically navigate and understand possible futures. He is also a regular contributor to Forbes and recently completed a ten-part series on the creation of sustainable wealth through interpreting environments as complex adaptive systems. In 2020 he also designed and delivered a multi-part Organizational Sciences Certification program with Forbes that was attended by executives from 250 companies. This program included a path-breaking approach to bringing about organizational change by leveraging light and was derived from Dr. Malik's 10-book series on Cosmology of Light.

Dr. Malik has held a number of leadership positions. He is currently Chief Strategy Officer at Galaxies, focused on modeling of complex realities, and Chief Technologist at Deep Order Technologies where he is spearheading the development of a revolutionary atom-based quantum computer. Dr. Malik has deep interest in core technologies such as quantum computing, artificial intelligence, genetics, and transhumanism. His recent writings propose alternative trajectories of development for each of these areas to increase the likelihood of sustainable global development. Formerly he has been Head of Organizational Sciences at Zappos.com - an eCommerce company, Managing Director of BSR - a global sustainability and environmental consulting company, and a member of the Founding Team of A.T. Kearney India - a global operations-focused management consulting company.

He has a Ph.D. in Technology Management with a focus on Mathematics of Innovation in Complex Adaptive Systems from the University of Pretoria, an MBA from Northwestern University's J.L. Kellogg Graduate School of Management with a focus on Marketing and Organizational Behavior, an MS in Computer Science from the University of Florida with a focus on AI, and a BSE in Computer Engineering from the Case Western Reserve University. He has also served on the faculty of Sri Aurobindo International Center of Education at the undergraduate level. Pravir is a global citizen who has lived, worked, and been educated in many parts of the world.

About the Illustrator

Margaret Astrid Phanes illustrates illuminating graphics of visual meditation. She teaches Light-Force meditation which has inspired these works. Ms. Phanes taught digital graphics at the University of Hawaii Maui College and the University of California, Santa Cruz. Her visual meditations on Light -Force consciousness have been presented at conferences, in international publications, and online. Her portfolio may be viewed at www.margaretphanes.com.

Selected Author Online Presence

- Amazon Author Page: https://www.amazon.com/Pravir-Malik/e/B002JVAEZE
- LinkedIn Profile: https://www.linkedin.com/in/pravirmalik/
- Forbes Page & Articles: https://www.forbes.com/sites/forbeshumanresourcescouncil/people/pravirmalik1/#1fa1097c17be
- Forbes Profile: https://profiles.forbes.com/members/hr/profile/Pravir-Malik-

- Head-Organizational-Sciences-Zappos/44463250-f2ab-434a-b1e2-0a6bdf54d970
- Google Scholar Page: https://scholar.google.com/citations?user=7DWWWZ8AAAAJ&hl=en
- Sage Author Page: https://us.sagepub.com/en-us/nam/author/pravir-malik
- IEEE Profile: https://ieeexplore.ieee.org/author/37086022058
- YouTube Page: https://www.youtube.com/user/Aurosoorya
- Twitter: https://twitter.com/PravirMalik
- Research Gate Profile: https://www.researchgate.net/profile/Pravir_Malik
- Eventbrite: https://www.eventbrite.com/o/pravir-malik-30159112262
- Medium: https://medium.com/@PravirMalik
- Company website: http://www.deepordertechnologies.com/

www.ingramcontent.com/pod-product-compliance
Lightning Source LLC
Chambersburg PA
CBHW042304150426
43197CB00001B/8